PRENTICE LITERATURE

PENGUIN EDITION

Standardized Test Preparation Workbook

Grade Six

PEARSON
Prentice Hall

Boston, Massachusetts
Upper Saddle River, New Jersey

PEARSON
Prentice Hall

ISBN 0-13-190795-6

1 2 3 4 5 6 7 8 9 10 05 06 07 08 09

Contents

Tests

Name ______________________ Date ____________

Screening Test

Directions: Read the following passages. Then read the questions. On the answer sheet, fill in the bubble for the answer that you think is correct.

Table of Contents

1 The chapter that gives information about water and weather begins on what page?

A 1
B 4
C 25
D 58

2 What topic is covered on page 77?

F Ocean Life
G Ocean Adventures
H Sea Monsters
J Swimming with Dolphins

Hundreds of years ago, the Incas of South America produced cloth unlike any the world has seen since. The Incas carefully bred animals called alpacas to get the finest, softest wool possible. Using the alpaca wool, the Incas wove colorful, silky cloth that was used for clothing, decorations, and even as money. When the Spaniards conquered the Incas, the secret to breeding the alpacas was lost.

3 What is the main idea of this paragraph?

A The Incas made a special kind of cloth.
B The Incas discovered how to breed alpacas.
C The Incas were conquered by the Spaniards.
D The Incas used colorful cloth as money.

Most of the world has been thoroughly explored, but scientists are still discovering large mammals. In 1993, scientists in Vietnam found the giant muntjac, a type of deer. The Chacoan peccary, a South American pig, was not identified until 1972. These discoveries give hope to people who believe that the forests of the world still hide unknown animals.

4 This paragraph is *mostly* about —

F the giant muntjac and other rare species
G the continuing discoveries of large mammals
H the exploration of South America and Vietnam
J the habitat and food of the Chacoan peccary

Name ______________________________ Date ______________

Jill looked at the clock and groaned. It was only eight o'clock on a Saturday morning. What was that awful hammering sound? She crawled out of bed and peeked outside. Seeing nothing, she closed the window with a thud. Then she snuggled back under the covers and tried to go back to sleep.

5 What causes Jill to close the window?

A Her room has gotten too cold.
B The sun is shining in her eyes.
C She is bothered by a noise outside.
D The traffic outside is too loud.

Max asked his mother if he could run with her in the morning. Max's mother was eager for a running partner, so she said yes. Max was surprised when his mother said they had to do some warm-up stretches first. She explained that their leg muscles might get sore if they didn't do the stretches. After they stretched, Max said his legs felt looser and he would be able to run better.

6 What is the effect of stretching?

F Both Max and his mother are able to run farther.
G Max's mother has a sore leg.
H Both Max and his mother run faster.
J Max's legs feel looser.

1 Animation was first used with toys in the 1800s. One of these toys was called the zoetrope, or wheel of life. A long paper strip covered with drawings was placed into the zoetrope's viewing tube. The user then peered through slots, twirled the tube, and watched the drawings move. This toy led to the first animated films.

2 In the 1920s, the Russians made animation with puppets. The Germans created animated films using dark shapes. Other countries experimented with frame-by-frame photographs of clay figures.

3 In the late 1920s, Walt Disney came on the scene. Disney created some of the best-loved animated movies of all time with characters such as Mickey Mouse, Donald Duck, Goofy, and Pluto.

7 Which of these is a *fact* about the zoetrope?

A It was the first animated film.
B It wasn't very much fun to watch.
C It was a toy that led to animation.
D It had a strange name.

8 Which of the following is an *opinion* from the passage?

F The Russians used puppets for their animation.
G The Germans created animated films using dark shapes.
H Other countries experimented with clay figures.
J Disney created the best-loved animated movies.

Name ______________________________ Date ______________

1 Sitting on a small triangle of land at the corner of Fifth Avenue and Broadway is one of the most interesting buildings in New York City. It is called the Flatiron Building.

2 The first thing people notice about the Flatiron Building is that it is built in a wedge shape. It looks like a tall piece of pie. It is only six feet wide at its round, narrow end. The building got its name from this shape. When it was built in 1902, it was called the Fuller Building. Its shape reminded people of an old-fashioned clothes iron. They started calling it the Flatiron Building, and the name stuck.

3 In 1902, there were very few tall buildings in New York City. The Flatiron Building was one of the first skyscrapers in the city. It is 285 feet high and has about 22 stories. At the time, that was huge. New Yorkers were afraid that a good gust of wind would blow this tall building over. That never happened, however. Today, the Flatiron Building looks tiny next to the huge skyscrapers in New York City. Even so, it is now the oldest skyscraper still standing in New York.

9 What do you learn in Paragraph 2 of this passage?

A where the Flatiron Building is located
B the shape of the Flatiron Building
C the height of the Flatiron Building
D how the Flatiron Building compares with other skyscrapers

10 Which words from the passage give the *best* description of the Flatiron Building?

F At the time, that was huge.
G It looks like a tall piece of pie.
H It is called the Flatiron Building.
J They started calling it the Flatiron Building, and the name stuck.

MOTHER: Harry, did you clean up your room?
HARRY: I guess it depends on what you mean by clean.
FATHER: Harry, would you please answer your mother?

11 What form of literature is this?

A Play
B Poem
C Fiction
D Nonfiction

12 Which of these is an example of fiction?

F the story of the first woman to fly a plane
G a book about how the Brooklyn Bridge was built
H a made-up story about animals that talk
J a book that tells you how to play soccer better

Name ______________________________ Date ______________

Directions: Read the following passages. Then read the questions. On the answer sheet, fill in the bubble for the answer that you think is correct.

1 The Celts were an ancient people who lived in Europe. During their reign, the Celts were feared and respected by the rest of the world.

2 Women in Celtic civilization had great freedom. Some Celtic women became important warriors and queens. The most famous Celtic queen was Boudicca. She led a rebellion against Roman rule.

3 At first, Boudicca and the Celts won many battles. They even destroyed the city of London, which was a Roman fortress then. Finally, however, the Romans defeated Boudicca and the Celts. No one knows exactly what happened to Boudicca. No matter what, she remains a symbol of Celtic power and freedom.

13 What is this story *mostly* about?

A ancient people who lived in Europe long ago
B a Celtic queen who battled the Romans
C why some Celtic women were warriors
D why London became a Roman fortress

14 The Romans defeated the Celts —

F after Boudicca was stripped of power
G after Boudicca and the Celts won many battles
H before Boudicca led a rebellion against Roman rule
J before Boudicca came to power

Corinne loved to play basketball, so she and her dad planned to build a basketball court. Corinne held the ladder steady, while her dad fastened a hoop and backboard to their garage. Then, they carefully measured and painted a free-throw line on the driveway. Corinne's dad smiled and said, "Well, champ, want to go one-on-one?"

15 Based on this paragraph, why does Corinne's dad help her with the basketball court?

A He wants to encourage Corinne to play basketball.
B He is tired of taking Corinne to basketball practice.
C He enjoys playing basketball with his friends.
D He thought it would be fun to do a project with Corinne.

There was once a scientist who believed that, if he studied the stars carefully enough, he could predict the future. The scientist went for long walks at night with his eyes fixed on the heavens. Refusing to take his eyes off the stars, the scientist tripped and fell into a deep, muddy hole. His cries for help attracted the villagers, who rescued him. One of them said, "You seek to read the future in the stars, but you fail to see what is at your feet!"

16 What lesson can be learned from this story?

F The wise do not let themselves be tricked twice.
G Do not count your chickens before they hatch.
H Hurry in the present, and regret it in the future.
J Do not let dreams of the future spoil the present.

Name ______________________ Date ______________

Favian Mercado thought it would be neat to run for student-body president, so he did. When the votes were counted, and Favian had won the election, he met with the vice principal to go over his new duties. Afterwards, Favian felt overwhelmed. He had no idea he would have to attend school-board meetings, write monthly reports, and organize the annual fundraiser. If he had known being president would be so much work, he might not have run.

17 The person telling this story is —

A Favian Mercado
B an outside narrator
C the current student-body president
D none of the above

18 The moral of this story is —

F nothing is worth more than freedom
G with greatness comes responsibility
H misfortune is the test of friendship
J common sense is a valuable treasure

Directions: Read each sentence. Choose the word that has the opposite meaning of the underlined word in the sentence. On the answer sheet, fill in the bubble for the answer that you think is correct.

19 My sister is always alert just before she plays in her soccer games.

A hungry
B dazed
C talkative
D nervous

20 Alex imagined what it would be like to live in a stone mansion with high ceilings and big windows.

F hut
G pasture
H cave
J castle

Directions: Read each sentence. Choose the word that has the same meaning as the underlined word in the sentence. On the answer sheet, fill in the bubble for the answer that you think is correct.

21 Victoria thought that it was absurd to have only one week to complete the term paper.

A intelligent
B ridiculous
C timely
D busy

22 Henri decided to combine all the ingredients for the brownies at the same time instead of adding the eggs last.

F sift
G purchase
H separate
J mix

Name ____________________ Date ____________

Directions: Look at this section of a dictionary on the right. Use this information to answer the questions below. On the answer sheet, fill in the bubble for the answer you think is correct.

23 According to the dictionary, the term "free and easy" means —

A without
B not under control of another
C release from bondage
D informal

24 The letters -ie in the word <u>freebie</u> are pronounced like the same letters in which of these words?

F Diet
G Lie
H Either
J Sieve

free (frē) ***adj.*** **fre•er, fre•est** [OE, *freo*] **1.** not under the control or power of another, having liberty, independent **2.** having civil liberties **3.** able to move in any direction; loose **4.** not burdened by obligations, discomforts, constraints, etc. **5.** not confined to the usual rules [*free* verse] **6.** not exact [a *free* translation] **7.** generous, profuse [*free* spending] **8.** with no charge or cost **9.** exempt from taxes, duties, etc. **10.** clear of obstructions [a *free* road] **11.** frank, straightforward **12.** open to all [a *free* port] **13.** not fastened ***—adv.*** **1.** without cost **2.** in a free manner ***—vt.*** **freed, free•ing** to make free; specif., *a)* to release from bondage, arbitrary power, obligation, etc. *b)* to clear of obstruction, etc. **—free and easy** informal **—free from** (or **of**) without **—make free** wish to use freely **—set free** to release; liberate **—freely** ***adv.***

free•bie, free•by (frē´ bē) ***n.*** *pl.* **–bies** [Slang] something given or gotten free of charge

Directions: Read the words below. Then look for mistakes in spelling. Fill in the bubble on the answer sheet that has the same letter as the mistake. If there is no mistake, fill in the last answer choice.

25 **A** anger
B trailer
C tracter
D *(No mistakes)*

26 **F** abuse
G spruce
H announce
J *(No mistakes)*

Directions: Read the sentences below. Then look for mistakes in capitalization. Fill in the bubble on the answer sheet that has the same letter as the mistake. If there is no mistake, fill in the last answer choice.

27 **A** Sarah and Carolyn
B want to attend Humphry
C College in september.
D *(No mistakes)*

28 **F** Michael picked
G out a new Book
H to read to his students.
J *(No mistakes)*

Name ______________________________ Date ______________

Practice Test 1

Answer the questions that follow.

1. Which of these is an example of simile?
   A. The children were exhausted.
   B. Her eyes were like jewels.
   C. The cymbals crashed noisily.
   D. He jumped into the icy lake.

2. Find the meaning of the underlined word in the sentence below.

   Most of the class considered Mr. Carter to be <u>dreamy</u>.

   A. attractive and wonderful
   B. tired and boring
   C. thoughtful and bright
   D. sleepy and withdrawn

Read the following selection. Then answer the questions that follow.

The Kitten

Margo and Fallon went to the old barn for the third day in a row. Quietly they slipped in through a hole on the side of the barn. There in the middle of the barn was a tiny ball of matted fur, lapping up milk from the bowl sitting in front of him.

"He's drinking it up!" Margo whispered with delight. The girls slowly moved forward. The kitten started. He looked up, saw the girls, and bolted up into the hayloft.

"He's too scared. Hell never trust us to take care of him," Margo said.

"I have one more idea. You wait here," said Fallon. She came back in a few minutes with a can of tuna. They took little pieces of tuna and made a path from the hayloft ladder to where they were standing. The kitten slowly began to follow the tuna trail. Finally he came cautiously near the girls. He sniffed and picked at each bite of tuna until he was eating out of their hands.

3. What is the setting of this story?
   A. a mountain cabin
   B. an old barn
   C. a seaside shack
   D. a haunted mansion

4. Why did the girls make a trail of tuna for the kitten?
   A. The kitten was supposed to be outside.
   B. They wanted the kitten to trust them.
   C. They wanted to see if the kitten liked tuna.
   D. They kitten was hungry and needed food.

Read the selection. Then answer the question that follows.

The New Girl

Students buzzed happily on their way to class, but Nina was alone. It was her first day at Comstock, and she wished it were her last.

Name ______________________________ Date ______________

In homeroom, Nina sat near a girl with red hair. The girl leaned over and whispered, "Hey, aren't you new?"

Nina nodded. The red-haired girl smiled and extended her hand. "I'm practically new. We moved here from Virginia two months ago."

The girl's name was Kaila, and by the time homeroom was over, a friendship had begun, and Nina felt much better about her new school.

5. What is the theme of this story?
   A. Feeling lonely is sometimes good.
   B. There is comfort in friendship.
   C. There is no friendship in a crowd.
   D. Real friends never let each other down.

Answer the questions that follow.

6. Which of these sentences ***probably*** came from a fairy tale?
   A. Atlantis was said to have existed long ago and to have been the site of an advanced civilization.
   B. Ulysses S. Grant had been unsuccessful at almost everything he tried.
   C. Flying across the ocean along was an enormous challenge that had cost several people their lives.
   D. The great troll stood up, sniffed the air, and then turned and walked into the forest.

7. What feeling is created in this line from a poem?

   Surrounded by fluffy, white clouds

   A. jealousy
   B. peacefulness
   C. anger
   D. anxiety

8. What type of image is created in these lines from a poem by Herman Melville?

   When ocean-clouds over inland hills
   Sweep storming in late autumn brown

   A. dismal
   B. cheerful
   C. scary
   D. busy

Read the following selection. Then answer the questions that follow.

Something Special for Mom

Isaac wanted to do something special for his mother, so he decided to make lasagna, her favorite dish. Laying out all the ingredients, Isaac checked to make sure he had everything the recipe called for.

"Oh no!" Isaac said to himself. He thought for a moment and then grabbed a small bowl and dashed out the front door. Within minutes he was back from Mrs. Arnold's house and carefully setting the bowl of eggs on the counter.

Name ______________________ Date ______________

9. Why did Isaac go to Mrs. Arnold's house?
   A. He needed to borrow eggs for the lasagna.
   B. He asked her for a recipe for lasagna.
   C. Mrs. Arnold showed him how to cook the pasta.
   D. Mrs. Arnold made some lasagna for Isaac.

10. Which of the following is an effect of Isaac wanting to do something special for his mother?
   A. Isaac realized that he did not have eggs.
   B. Isaac decided to make lasagna.
   C. Isaac went to Mrs. Arnold's house.
   D. Isaac grabbed a small bowl.

Read the following selection. Then answer the questions that follow.

Owning a Pet

Owning a pet teaches responsibility. Pets require regular feeding, grooming, and sometimes walking and playing. Some pets live in cages. Their cages must be cleaned and the cage lining must be replaced. Certain animals need special care. Horses wear shoes that must be cared for. Fish must have clean water to swim in. Some fish even need to live in water that stays at a certain temperature. When pet owners go on trips, they must plan for the care of their pets while they are gone. A person can learn a lot from owning a pet.

11. Which of the following is the ***best*** summary of the selection?
   A. Some pets have cages that must be cleaned.
   B. Horses wear shoes that must be cared for.
   C. People must take their pets with them on trips.
   D. The various tasks involved in pet ownership teach people responsibility.

12. Which of the following conclusions can you draw from this selection?
   A. Dogs are easier to care for than fish.
   B. People who own horses are the most responsible pet owners.
   C. Caring for a pet can be hard work.
   D. Animals that live in cages don't make good pets.

Read the following selection. Then answer the questions that follow.

Lessons Learned

For years, the huge old Andrews place has sat empty in a weedy lot. It had once been a grand home, but now it was a wreck. The Main Street Historical Society wanted to turn the house into a museum. The members held bake sales and flea markets to raise money, but still there wasn't enough. The society wrote to the newspaper for help.

The next meeting of the Historical Society was packed with people. Maddie Rose, the society's president, was surprised. The room was filled with kids! Most of the group's members were older, and many of them were grandparents. They had never seen kids at their meetings before.

Name ______________________________ Date ______________

When the meeting started, a smiling young girl stood up. "My name is Sarah Wilson, and these are my friends," she said. "We are in the sixth grade and saw your letter in the newspaper. We've been studying city history in class. We'd like to help you fix the Andrews House."

Many society members were against the idea. They didn't believe that a bunch of kids could be of any help. One member, Fred Thompson, was especially against the idea. Over his objections, the society agreed to let the kids help.

The next day, Saturday, was clean-up day at the Andrews House. Maddie arrived early. The place was swarming with kids and society members. Together, they were pulling out the weeds, raking the yard, and hauling away trash. The place buzzed with activity, and everyone seemed to be having a good time.

Fred saw Maddie and walked over to her. He said sheepishly, "I never would have believed that kids could do this much good."

Maddie smiled. She knew better. "Now what do you think of letting kids help out?"

13. From the information in the selection, what can you infer about Sarah?
- **A.** She was against the idea of helping at first.
- **B.** She probably helped organize the students.
- **C.** She never helped out like this before.
- **D.** She really didn't like Fred Thompson.

14. How do Maddie's and Fred's attitudes toward the kids differ before the end of the selection?
- **A.** Fred thinks the kids will be a big help to the society.
- **B.** Maddie thinks the kids may try to steal things from the Andrews House.
- **C.** Maddie doesn't think that the kids will work hard enough.
- **D.** Fred doesn't think that the kids would be much of a help to the society.

15. What assumption about kids does the author of this selection make?
- **A.** Kids are always ready to help out for a good cause.
- **B.** Kids are only good for cleaning up messes.
- **C.** Kids don't read newspapers often enough.
- **D.** Kids work harder than anyone else.

Read the following selection. Then answer the questions that follow.

The Forbidden City

The Forbidden City in Beijing, China, is the largest palace complex in the world. Set in the middle of Beijing, it covers and area of 720,000 square meters and even has a moat around the outside for protection.

For almost 500 years the Forbidden City housed the emperors of China. The buildings of the city were home to the emperor's family and were also the area from which the emperor and his officials ruled the country. The city was closed to all but the highest government and military officials. Today, the city has been renamed the Palace museum and is open to the public.

Name ________________________________ Date ________________

It took 15 years to complete the palace, which was started during the Ming Dynasty. According to Chinese records, over one million workers were needed to build the city. It was made from wood and brick. The main color used n all the buildings was yellow, even though he official name of the city was the Purple Forbidden City. Yellow is the color most closely linked to emperors, and in the Forbidden City all but one building has a yellow tile roof.

The Forbidden City now consists of more than ten different museums for the art within the palace and the records held there. The city is China's largest museum, housing about one million objects, many of which are one of a kind. Although the palace is no longer the ruling center of China, it still has an impact on the many people who visit every day.

16. What is the purpose of this selection?
- **A.** to persuade readers to visit China
- **B.** to describe what life was like for an ancient Chinese emperor
- **C.** to inform readers about the Forbidden City in Beijing, China
- **D.** to entertain readers with an amusing story about life in Beijing, China

17. What question is left unanswered by the third paragraph?
- **A.** What was used to build the palace?
- **B.** How long did it take to build the palace?
- **C.** What was the main color used in the Forbidden City?
- **D.** Why was the city named the Purple Forbidden City?

18. Why was the palace complex known as the Forbidden City?
- **A.** People, except for important officials, were not allowed to enter the city.
- **B.** People were not allowed to speak while inside the city.
- **C.** The emperor's family was not allowed to leave the city.
- **D.** People were not allowed to bring weapons into the city.

Read the following selection. Then answer the questions that follow.

Who Invented Band-Aids®?

Although many people don't even know his name, Earle Dickson was responsible for creating one of today's most common household items. Dickson was the genius behind Band-Aids®.

In 1917, Dickson was a newly married man a cotton buyer for a successful bandage company in New Jersey called Johnson & Johnson. As the story goes, Dickson's wife, Frances, was accident-prone. She often cut herself or nicked her fingers doing various household tasks. The regular bandages were too big and clumsy for Frances, so Dickson devised something better.

He folded pads of cotton gauze and place them on long strings of surgical tape. He covered this with a material called *crinoline*. This prevented the tape from sticking to itself when it was rolled back together. Frances could unroll the bandage and cut off as much as she needed.

Name ______________________________ Date ______________

One day, Dickson mentioned his creation to a friend at work. Soon, Dickson was before the Johnsons, showing them what he had come up with. The Johnsons were especially impressed by the fact that you could put the new bandage on yourself. Up to that point, bandages had been difficult to apply without help.

Johnson & Johnson began producing Band-Aids®, but the bandages didn't take off until the mid-1920s when the company gave thousands of samples to the Boy Scouts. After that, Band-Aids® were a hit. Dickson was made vice president of Johnson & Johnson, and when he died in 1961, the company was selling $30,000,000 dollars' worth of Band-Aids® a year.

19. How did bandages differ before and after the creation of Band-Aids®?
   - A. Regular bandages were much less expensive than Band-Aids®.
   - B. Regular bandages were difficult to apply without help, unlike Band-Aids®.
   - C. Regular bandages were smaller and less clumsy than Band-Aids®.
   - D. Regular bandages were only given out by doctors, but Band-Aids® were sold in stores.

20. If you were writing a comparison-and-contrast essay about how bandages differed before and after the creation of Band-Aids®, which of the following would be the ***best*** pre-writing plan method?
   - A. Venn diagram
   - B. word web
   - C. story map
   - D. character-image map

21. If you were taking notes about this passage, which of the following would belong?
   - A. Dickson invented crinoline.
   - B. Band-Aids® were popular right away.
   - C. Early bandages were easy to apply.
   - D. Dickson worked for Johnson & Johnson.

22. Which of the following sentences from the passage shows the author's bias toward Dickson?
   - A. One day, Dickson mentioned his creation to a friend at work.
   - B. Up to that point, bandages had been difficult to apply without help.
   - C. Dickson was the genius behind Band-Aids®.
   - D. He covered this with a material called *crinoline.*

Read the following article written by a student about a recent change in school policy. Then answer the questions that follow.

Requirement is Unfair to Athletes

At its meeting last week, the school board decided to require student athletes to attend Physical Education (P.E.) classes. As an athlete, I feel this requirement is unfair.

Playing a team sport at school requires the same type of activity (physical exercise) as a P.E. course. Athletes may exhaust or injure themselves if they take part in both activities. In addition, the time spent in P.E. courses can be put to use by coaches as training time. That way, athletes would not have to spend so much time training after school and would have more time to study. This is especially important for athletes because they are not usually good students. Finally, as I understand it, P.E. courses are supposed to develop an interest in athletics. Students who take part in team sports already have this interest. For athletes, P.E. is unnecessary, and it might even be harmful—both physically and academically.

I hope our school district will consider the time and effort student athletes put into their teams and reconsider its decision.

23. Why was this article written?

- **A.** to complain about athletic teams
- **B.** to persuade the school board to change its decision
- **C.** to explain why the school board made its decision
- **D.** to describe the school's physical education program

24. What does the writer mean when she says that P.E. classes would be academically harmful for athletes?

- **A.** P.E. classes would be difficult for athletes and they might fail.
- **B.** P.E. classes take up time athletes could use to study for their other classes.
- **C.** Athletes who take P.E. classes would have to drop out of one of their other courses.
- **D.** P.E. classes would create too much homework for athletes.

25. Which of the following statements from the article is an example of stereotype?

- **A.** This is especially important for athletes because they are not usually good students.
- **B.** As an athlete, I feel this requirement is unfair.
- **C.** Athletes may exhaust or injure themselves if they take part in both activities.
- **D.** I hope our school district will consider the time and effort student athletes put into their teams and reconsider its decision.

Name ______________________________ Date ______________

Practice Test 2

Read the following passages. Then answer the questions that follow.

Encyclopedia Entry

The word *sabotage* comes from the French word *sabot.* A sabot is a wooden shoe. The commonly accepted origin, or history, of this word is as follows: During the Industrial Revolution, French factory workers became concerned about their future. They were worried about the possibility of losing their jobs because of new automated machinery. To avoid this possibility, the workers threw their wooden shoes into their machines so that the machines would break down. To throw a wooden shoe into a machine became known as sabotage, or the act of destroying property or plans on purpose. A saboteur is someone who causes sabotage.

Dictionary Entry

sab-o-tage (sab′ täzh) *n.* 1. any interference with production work in a plant or factory, especially by enemy agents or employees during a work dispute 2. any undermining of a cause *v.* to injure or attack by sabotage

History Book

Sabotage is considered by many to be one of the most terrible crimes. The act of sabotage is sneaky at best. At worst, it makes the person committing the crime a traitor. Although it was given its name during the Industrial Revolution, sabotage has been with us for thousands of years. It is likely that enslaved workers in Roman and Egyptian times used sabotage at least occasionally. In more modern times, sabotage has been a tool of warfare. It is hated by the side against whom the sabotage is committed. The side that causes the sabotage, however, sees it as a noble act.

1. Which information source gives the most complete information about sabotage?
   - A. the encyclopedia entry
   - B. they dictionary entry
   - C. the history book
   - D. They all give the same information.

2. If you were writing a report about the history of sabotage, which of the following could you use as a primary source?
   - A. an encyclopedia entry about sabotage
   - B. a journal entry from a 19th century saboteur
   - C. a section from a social studies textbook about sabotage
   - D. a movie about sabotage in a metal factory

Read the following selection. Then answer the questions that follow.

The Sahara is the largest desert in the world. __1__ in northern Africa, it covers more than three million square miles. It is one of the most difficult places on Earth in which to live. Despite this, __2__ consider it one of the most beautiful places on Earth.

3. Choose the word that belongs in space (1).
   - A. Locater
   - B. Locating
   - C. Located
   - D. Was located

Name ______________________________ Date ______________

4. Choose the word that belongs in space (2).

A. some
B. somebody
C. anybody
D. both

Answer the questions that follow.

5. Choose the word that best completes the following sentence:

The carpenter's carving of the bear was done ________.

A. skill
B. skillfulness
C. skillful
D. skillfully

6. Which of the following words is spelled correctly?

A. ceiling
B. cieling
C. ceeling
D. cealing

Read the following selection. Then answer the questions that follow.

Franklin Delano Roosevelt

(1) Historians believe that Franklin Delano Roosevelt was among the greatest American presidents. (2) During his terms in office, Roosevelt successfully faced two enormous challenges. (3) The Great Depression and World War II. (4) Their ability to deal with these events was recognized by the voters. (5) He one the presidency four times, a feat that no previous president had ever accomplished.

7. Which change should be made to correct sentence 1?

A. change ***american*** to ***American***
B. change ***Roosevelt*** to ***Roosevelt,***
C. change ***presidents*** to ***president***
D. change ***believe*** to ***believes***

8. Which of the following is a fragment?

A. (1) Historians believe that Franklin Delano Roosevelt was among the greatest American presidents.
B. (3) The Great Depression and World War II.
C. (4) Their ability to deal with these events was recognized by the voters.
D. (5) He one the presidency four times, a feat that no previous president had ever accomplished.

9. Which change should be made to correct sentence 4?

A. change ***Their*** to ***His***
B. change ***ability*** to ***abilities***
C. change ***was*** to ***were***
D. change ***events*** to ***events,***

10. Which change should be made to correct sentence 5?

A. change ***He*** to ***Him***
B. change ***one*** to ***won***
C. change ***accomplished.*** to ***accomplished?***
D. change ***had*** to ***has***

Name ______________________________ Date ______________

Read the following sentences. Then answer the question that follows.

(1) On calm days, cooking is a breeze.

(2) Jake as an unusual job.

(3) People always ask what it's like to cook at sea.

(4) But when the seas become violent, and the boat is tossed up and down and side to side, cooking can be a challenge.

(5) Jake says that it depends on the weather.

(6) He is a cook for a crew of five on a tugboat.

11. Which of the following reflects the ***best*** organization for the sentences above?

A. 3, 5, 6, 1, 2, 4
B. 1, 2, 5, 4, 3, 6
C. 2, 6, 3, 5, 1, 4
D. 6, 4, 2, 1, 3, 5

Answer the questions that follow.

12. Which of the following is the *best* way to revise this sentence?

Believing that poets are just like everyone else, William Wordsworth also thought that they are a little more sensitive to their surroundings.

A. William Wordsworth believed that poets are just like everyone else, except that they are a little more sensitive to their surroundings.
B. William Wordsworth believed that everyone else is sensitive like poets.
C. William Wordsworth believed that poets were like everyone else, sensitive to their surroundings.
D. William Wordsworth believed that everyone else was insensitive, while poets were more sensitive.

13. Which of the following sentences *best* demonstrates the relationship between ideas?

A. Alex wanted to go to the farmer's market, and it was closed on Thursdays.
B. Alex wanted to go to the farmer's market, or it was closed on Thursdays.
C. Alex wanted to go to the farmer's market, but it was closed on Thursdays.
D. Alex wanted to go to the farmer's market, so it was closed on Thursdays.

Suppose that you and several of your classmates must work in a small group to create an oral presentation convincing classmates about the importance of eating nutritious foods. Each group member must participate. Answer the questions that follow.

14. In your oral presentation, which of the following would you *most* likely include?

A. figurative language
B. a friend's opinion
C. persuasive language
D. complex technical language

Name ______________________ Date ______________

15. Which of the following would be an inappropriate comment during a discussion about nutrition?

A. My favorite nutritious snack is fruit.
B. Many people don't have the time to cook nutritious foods.
C. I think it's important to eat healthful foods.
D. Nutrition is stupid.

16. Which of the following would be the best way to approach the presentation?

A. complete the research, write the presentation, create the visual aids
B. write the presentation, complete the research, create the visual aids
C. create the visual aids, write the presentation, complete the research
D. create the visual aids, complete the research, write the presentation

17. Which of the following behaviors would be the most appropriate while participating in a group activity?

A. ignoring other group members
B. arguing with the group leader
C. listening to the other group members
D. making fun of the other group members' opinions

The following two viewpoints were presented during a debate. Read the passages. Then answer the questions that follow.

Soccer is the most physically challenging sport one can play. In order to play soccer well, one must be in top condition.

Unlike soccer, tennis involves both the upper and lower body, giving the participant a total physical workout. Tennis requires strength, balance, coordination, and endurance. In addition, it requires mental focus and knowledge of strategy. That is why some of the best athletes in the world are tennis players.

18. Which of the following is a *fact* from the debate?

A. Tennis involves both the upper and lower body.
B. In order to pay soccer well, one must be in top condition.
C. Some of the best athletes in the world are tennis players.
D. Soccer is the most physically challenging sport one can play.

19. Of the two viewpoints above, which is the more convincing?

A. the first viewpoint
B. the second viewpoint
C. Neither viewpoint is convincing.
D. Both viewpoints are equally convincing.

Name ______________________________ Date ______________

Answer the following questions.

20. Which of the following is the *most* appropriate way to paraphrase information given in an oral presentation?

A. copy the speaker's presentation word for word

B. restate the information in your own words

C. quote the speaker directly

D. borrow language from the speaker

21. Which type of language would be the *least* appropriate to use in a formal presentation?

A. technical

B. persuasive

C. scientific

D. casual

Read the following speech. Then answer the questions that follow.

The Park Action Committee (PAC) was started in 1979 to make sure that parks and wildlife would be protected. Many parks were in danger of becoming littered beyond help, and local wildlife was eating plastic bags and aluminum foil left behind by park guests. PAC has improved the national parks and kept animals safe for over 20 years. We ask the state of Montana to consider giving us money so that we can keep doing the job we do. Help PAC to help you by funding out projects this year.

22. If you were giving this speech, which of the following statements would be the best addition to help convince the state of Montana to give PAC money?

A. Give PAC more money now!

B. Without PAC's help, Montana's parks will not receive as many visitors, and its wildlife will not thrive.

C. If all of its wildlife dies, it will be the state of Montana's fault, not PAC's.

D. If Montana doesn't give PAC money, something really bad could happen.

23. Which is the *best* summary of the speech above?

A. The Park Action Committee (PAC) needs funding from the state of Montana to continue its dedication to cleaning national parks and protecting wildlife.

B. The Park Action Committee (PAC) needs help from the state of Montana to pick up litter.

C. The Park Action Committee (PAC) wants to create more parks for Montana's wildlife.

D. The Park Action Committee (PAC) wants wildlife to stop eating aluminum foil.

Name ______________________________ Date ______________

Answer the following questions.

24. Suppose you need to include sensory details in a story that you are writing. Which of the following sentences should you choose?

A. The school cafeteria line a busy, happy place at lunchtime.

B. Students shrieked with laughter and shouted happily as they snaked through the cafeteria line.

C. It was loud in the cafeteria, and there were lots and lots of students in line.

D. We all talked and laughed as we went through the cafeteria line.

25. Read the dictionary entry below. Other than *-s*, what ending would you add to make *tableau* plural?

tab•leau *n, pl* tab•leaux *also* tableaus

[origin: F, fr. MF *tablel*] 1: a graphic description or representation

A. -ion

B. -x

C. -el

D. -ses

Name ______________________________ Date ______________

Practice Test 3

"Career Connections Athletic Coaches

1) Squeaky is the fastest runner in her neighborhood, and she makes a real effort to train herself for her races. She might be an even faster runner, however, if she had a track coach to guide her training.

2) Athletic coaches can help make the difference between a good athlete and a great one. They teach beginners the fundamentals of a sport, lead athletes through a season, and help world champions sharpen their skills. Coaches and instructors also help amateurs who simply want to increase their personal enjoyment of a sport or improve their exercise routine.

3) Coaches can be found guiding teams and individuals at the professional and Olympic levels, at schools and colleges, and even at local fitness centers, ice rinks, and swimming pools. The nature of the work of all athletic coaches is to teach. As a result, they must be knowledgeable in their respective sports, keep up with the latest procedures and techniques, and develop an effective teaching method to share the information with their athletes.

4) Coaches at all levels must also be concerned with safety, ensuring that each athlete knows the proper methods of using equipment and maximizing performance without causing injury

5) Athletic coaches at public and private schools are usually required to have a bachelor's degree from an accredited college or university. Sports instructors may not have a college or university degree, but they are usually skillful players of a particular sport.

6) If you are considering a career as an athletic coach or instructor, a great way to start preparing is to participate in sports now.

1. Which of the following is best supported by the selection?
- **A.** Coaches must continue to teach.
- **B.** Coaches must be professional athletes.
- **C.** Coaches must continually study their sport to be effective.
- **D.** Coaches must be in peak condition to be effective teachers.

2. Why do coaches need to be concerned with safety?
- **A.** to keep their licenses
- **B.** to keep good jobs.
- **C.** to protect their schools and colleges.
- **D.** To protect the athletes they are coaching.

3. Why are some coaches required to have a college degree?
- **A.** because they are teachers.
- **B.** because they have to play college sports.
- **C.** because they have to be smart.
- **D.** because they will be better coaches

4. Which of the following relationship is most similar to the relationship below?
coaches : athletes
- **A.** mothers: fathers
- **B.** teachers : students
- **C.** students : teachers
- **D.** fathers : mothers

Name ______________________________ Date ______________

A Noiseless Patient Spider

By Walt Whitman

1) A noiseless patient spider,
2) I marked where on a promontory it stood isolated,
3) Marked how to explore the vacant vast surroundings,
4) It launched forth filament, filament, filament out of itself,
5) Ever unreeling them,ever tirelessly speeding them.
6) And you O my soul where you stand, Surrounded, detached, in measureless oceans of space,
7) Ceaselessly musing, venturing, throwing, seeking the spheres to connect them,
8) Till the bridge you will need be formed,
9) Till the ductile anchor hold,
10) Till the gossamer thread you fling catch somewhere, O my soul.

5. Based on the context of the poem, what is the meaning of *marked?*

A. pushed
B. watched
C. listened
D. moved

6. What was the spider doing in stanza 1?

A. climbing a wall
B. catching a bug
C. building a web
D. exploring a space

7. In stanza 2 the author compare the spiders web to which of the following?

A. bridges
B. his soul
C. his thoughts
D. thread

8. What is the main idea of the poem?

A. Spiders and people are a lot alike.
B. Spiders work very hard when building a large web.
C. People are lonely like spiders.
D. People must keep tying to understand themselves.

9. Which of the following relationshipsis most like the relationship below?

filaments : threads

A. thoughts : ideas
B. teachers : students
C. books : school
D. religions : beliefs

Name ______________________________ Date ________________

"The Talking Stone"

from *The Hungry Woman: Myths and Legends of the Aztecs,*

edited by John Bierhorst

MEXICO

1) The Aztec empire was at its greatest under the rule of Montezuma in the early 1500's. Still, there were signs that the end of the empire might be near. One of these signs was described in the legend of the talking stone.

2) Montezuma wanted the monuments that he built to be the most beautiful in Mexico's history. None of the beautiful things that the previous kings had built were good enough. He said, "Not splendid enough for Mexico." He decided that the large round stone that was used to sacrifice prisoners to the god, Huitzilopochtli, must be replaced with a larger more beautiful stone. He said, " the stone must be a forearm wide and two forearms taller."

3) He sent his finest stonecutters to the country side to look for the perfect stone. When one was found he sent for mend from six cities who could help lift and haul the stone.

4) Using their levers, they pried the stone from the hillside and dragged it to a level spot to be carved. As soon as it was in position, thirty stonecutters began to chisel it with their flint chisels, making it not only bigger than any round -stone that had been seen before, but more unusual and more beautiful.

5) During the time that they worked, they ate only the rarest delicacies, sent by Montezuma and served by the people of Acolco.

6) When the stone was ready to be taken to Mexico, the carvers sent word to the king, who ordered the temple priests to go bring incense and a supply of quails. Arriving at the stone, the priests decorated it with paper streamers, perfumed it with the incense, and spattered molten rubber. Then they twisted the necks of the quails and spattered quail blood. There were musicians, too, with conch horns and skin drums. And comedians also came, so that the stone could be entertained as it traveled along.

7) But when they tried to pull it, it would not be moved. It seemed to have grown roots, and all the ropes snapped as if they had been cotton threads. Two more cities were ordered to send haulers, and as they set to work, shouting back and forth, trussing it with fresh ropes, the stone spoke up and said,
"Try what you will."

8) Suddenly the shouting stopped. "*Why do you pull me?*" said the stone. "*I am not about to turn over and go, I am not to be pulled where you want me to go.*" Quietly the men kept working. "*Then pull me,*" it said. "*I'll talk to you later.*" And with that the stone slid forward, traveling easily as far as Tlapitzahuayan.

9) There the haulers decided to rest for the day, while two stonecutters went ahead to warn Montezuma that the great stone had begun to talk. "*Are you drunk?*" said the king when they gave him the news. "Why come here telling me lies?" Then he called for his storekeeper and had the two messengers locked up. But he sent six lords to find out the truth, and when they had heard the stone say, "*Try what you will, I am not to be pulled,*" they went back to Mexico and reported it to Montezuma, and the two prisoners were set free.

10) In the morning the stone spoke again. " *Will you never understand? Why do you pull me? I am not to be taken to Mexico. Tell Montezuma it is no use. The time is bad, and his end is near. He has tried to make himself greater than our lord who created the sky and the earth. But pull me if you*

Name ______________________________ Date ______________

must, you poor ones. Let's go." And with that the stone slid along until it reached Itztapalapan. Again it halted, and again they sent messengers to tell Montezuma what it had said. Just as before, he flew into a rage, but this time he was secretly frightened, and although he refused to give the messengers credit for bringing him the truth, he stopped short of jailing them and told them to go back and carry out his orders.

11) The next morning, as the haulers picked up their ropes, they found that the stone once again moved easily, sliding as far as the causeway that led to Mexico. Advised that the stone had reached the other side of the water, Montezuma sent priests to greet it with flowers and incense, also to appease it with blood sacrifices in case it might be angry. Again it started to move. But when it was halfway across the lake, it stopped and said, *"Here and no farther,"* and although the causeway was made of cedar beams seven hands thick, the stone broke through them, crashing into the water with a noise like thunder.

12) All the men who were tied to the ropes were dragged down and killed, and many others were wounded. Told what had happened, Montezuma himself came onto the causeway to see where the stone had disappeared.

13) Still thinking he would carry out his plan, he ordered divers to search the bottom of the lake to see if the stone had settled in a place where it might be hauled back to dry land. But they could find neither the stone itself nor any sign of the men who had been killed. The divers were sent down a second time, and when they came back up they said, *"Lord, we see a narrow trace in the water leading toward Acolco." "Very well,"* said Montezuma, and with no further questioning he sent his stonecutters back to Acolco to see what they might discover, and when they returned, they reported no more than what the king already knew.

14) Still tied with its ropes and spattered with incense and blood offerings, the stone had gone back to the hillside where it had originally been found. Then Montezuma turned to his lords and said, *"Brothers, I know now that our pains and troubles will be many and our days will be few. As for me, just as the*

15) Why most likely did Montezuma kings that have gone before, I must let myself die. May the Lord of Creation do what he pleases."

Name ______________________ Date ______________

10. Based on the context of paragraph 2, who *most likely* was Huitzilopochtli?

A. an emperor
B. a monument
C. a pagan god
D. a sacred stone

11. Why *most likely* did Montezuma describe what he wanted using a forearm?

A. It described the causeway
B. It was a unit of measurement
C. He had large forearms
D. He did not know how to measure.

12. Why *most likely* were haulers summoned from six cities?

A. The haulers were stronger than other workers.
B. The haulers were stronger than Montezuma's workers
C. The stone was very large
D. The stone said it would not be moved.

13. Why *most likely* did Montezuma provide the best food for the stonecutters?

A. That was the only way to get them to work
B. They insisted on good food.
C. He wanted them to do their best work.
D. He was famous for providing good food.

14. Why *most likely* did Montezuma imprison the stonecutters?

A. He was mad at them
B. He thought they were making excuses.
C. He didn't believe the stone could talk.
D. He thought they were stupid.

15. Why *most likely* did the stone allow the workers to move him even part of the way?

A. The stone could not make up his mind.
B. The stone was very tired.
C. The stone wanted to go.
D. The stone felt sorry for the workers.

16. What is the main idea of the selection?

A. Emperors don't always get their way.
B. Magic stones cannot be trusted.
C. Even determination is not always enough.
D. Punishing workers is not good.

Name ______________________________ Date ______________

Let's Make a Piñata

Most people think of children's parties in Mexico when they hear the word Piñata, but according to legend, the Piñata was actually introduce to the West by Marco Polo who learned of them in China. Piñata's are hollow paper shapes usually formed to look like animals. They are filled with candy and trinkets. The fun starts when children are given a small bat which is used to bash the shape until is crumbles and all the goodies fall to the floor. The following is a recipe for making your own piñata. It is easy and fun.

Needed Materials:
1 Round balloon
Plenty of Newspaper
Water
Flour
Glue
Scissors
Crepe paper

Steps:

1) Inflate your balloon. It will form the body of your piñata, so inflate it to the size you want your piñata to be.

2) Cover the floor with newspaper to prevent a big mess.

3.) Fill a large bowl ¾ full of flour, and then add water until you have a thick mixture the consistency of wallpaper paste.

4.) Tear newspaper into strips that are about 2 inches wide. Dip the newspaper strips into the mixture. You have just made paper Mache! Make sure that the newspaper is totally saturated, but not dripping, and begin to lay the strips over the balloon. Continue until the balloon is covered in a thick layer of paper Mache.

5.) Let the balloon dry until it is stiff and no longer sticky. This may take overnight.

6.) When the paper Mache shape if dry glue colorful crepe paper to the outside and decorate your piñata in a creative way.

7.) This step is best done with the help of an adult! Using a serrated knife, cut a rectangular flap in one side of the piñata. Fill the cavity with candy, confetti, and (if you want) small toys. Then tape the flap shut. You can add more crepe paper to cover the flap.

Tips:

* Punch two small holes in the top of your Piñata and pass a string through the holes so that you can hang it.

* If you want your Pinata to have a traditional look you should attach paper streamers to each side.

* Remember that this is your creation. You don't have to limit your decorations to crepe paper. You can add glitter, feathers, fake flowers…whatever you like.

* It is best to use wrapped candy. Remember that all the goodies will be falling to the floor.

* A piñata add fun to any party or family occasion. You could make an Easter egg or a jack lantern or a fat reindeer. Use your imagination

Name ______________________ Date ______________

17. Why is it necessary to spread newspaper on the floor before you begin the project?
- **A.** You can't make the piñata without newspaper.
- **B.** Newspaper makes the best piñatas
- **C.** It will make it easier to clean up.
- **D.** It is the only way to complete the project.

18. Why is it necessary to inflate the balloon?
- **A.** You have to create a cavity.
- **B.** You could pop the balloon.
- **C.** The balloon is too large.
- **D.** The balloon will not come out.

19. Why *most likely* would you want the piñata to have a sturdy string
- **A.** A weak string looks bad.
- **B.** A weak string will break too easily.
- **C.** Children will be hitting the piñata with a bat.
- **D.** Children will cut the string.

20. Why *most likely* do most people think pinata's started in Mexico?
- **A.** Because they have read it in books.
- **B.** Because they are seen most often at Mexican parties.
- **C.** Because they are Mexican.
- **D.** Because all Mexican children have piñatas.

21. Why *most likely* do the directions tell you to use your imagination
- **A.** Because it is an art project.
- **B.** Because no two should look alike.
- **C.** Becausc you should not copy other people.
- **D.** Because it is more fun.

22. What is paper Mache?
- **A.** a Mexican tool
- **B.** a serrated knife
- **C.** newspaper and paste
- **D.** a Mexican glue

Name ______________________________ Date ______________

Ain't I a Woman?

Sojourner Truth

Sojourner Truth was born Isabella Baumfree in New York state in 1797. As a slave she was sold several times and endured many hardships. In 1828 New York abolished slavery and as a free woman Isabella changed her name. She traveled on foot through New York and Connecticut preaching emancipation and women's rights. She never had the benefit of an education; however, she was a powerful speaker. She died in1883, but her ideas have lived on.

1) Well, children, where there is so much racket there must be something out of kilter. I think that 'twixt the Negroes of the South and the women at the North, all talking about rights, the white men will be in a fix pretty soon. But what's all this here talking about?

2) That man over there says that women need to be helped into carriages, and lifted over ditches, and to have the best place everywhere. Nobody ever helps me into carriages, or over mud-puddles, or gives me any best place! And ain't I a woman?

3) Look at me! Look at my arm! I have ploughed and planted, and gathered into barns, and no man could head me! And ain't I a woman? I could work as much and eat as much as a man-when I could get it-and bear the lash as well! And ain't I a woman?

4) I have borne thirteen children, and seen them most all sold off to slavery, and when I cried out with my mother's grief, none but Jesus heard me! And ain't I a woman?

5) Then they talk about this thing in the head; what's this they call it? [Intellect, someone whispers.] That's it, honey. What's that got to do with women's rights or Negro's rights? If my cup won't hold but a pint, and yours holds a quart, wouldn't you be mean not to let me have my little half-measure full?

6) Then that little man in black there, he says women can't have as much rights as men, 'cause Christ wasn't a woman! Where did your Christ come from? Where did your Christ come from? From God and a woman! Man had nothing to do with Him. If the first woman God ever made was strong enough to turn the world upside down all alone, these women together ought to be able to turn it back, and get it right side up again!

7) And now they is asking to do it, the men better let them. Obliged to you for hearing me, and now old Sojourner ain't got nothing more to say.

Name ______________________ Date ______________

23. Based on the context of paragraph 1, what is the meaning of '*twixt*?
A. beside
B. according
C. between
D. available

24. Why *most likely* did the author repeat the words, "Ain't I a woman?"
A. to make her work rhyme
B. to show she was a woman
C. to protect women's rights
D. to point out injustice

25. Who *most likely* is the little man in black in paragraph 6?
A. a politician
B. a policeman
C. a minister
D. a soldier

26. Why *most likely* was the word intellect not in Sojourners vocabulary?
A. She forgot the word.
B. She could not read.
C. She had never heard the word.
D. She was not an educated person.

27. Why *most likely* was Sojourner concerned about women's rights?
A. Her life had been very hard.
B. She had been a slave.
C. She had traveled through the North.
D. Her family had been sold into slavery

28. What *most likely* was Truth referencing with her figurative language in paragraph 5?
A. black versus. white
B. men versus women
C. ability to speak
D. ability to learn

29. Which of the following relationships is most similar to the relationship below?
Truth : women's rights
A. ministers: men
B. King : civil rights
C. women : parents
D. Lincoln : Civil War

30. What is the main idea of the selection?
A. All black women should be free.
B. All men should give women their rights.
C. Women should have equal rights with men.
D. All blacks should be free.

31. Why *most likely* was the selection
A. to make it more interesting.
B. to let the reader know how Truth spoke.
C. to make the selection funny
D. to show that Truth had very little schooling

Name ______________________ Date ______________

from The Phantom Tollbooth

by Susan Nanus based on the book by Norton Juster

The Phantom Tollbooth is a fantasy. Milo, a young boy, is bored with his life. He is in a rut. It seems that he does the same things over and over again. Suddenly a phantom tollbooth becomes a part of his life and everything changes. His life becomes one great adventure.

Act I Scene 1

Cast: Clock Milo A Voice

[The stage is completely dark and silent. Suddenly the sound of someone winding an alarm clock is heard, and after that, the sound of loud ticking is hear.]

[LIGHTS UP on the CLOCK, a huge alarm clock. The CLOCK reads 4:00. The lighting should make it appear that the CLOCK ticks for 30 seconds]

CLOCK. See that! Half a minute gone by. Seems like a long time when you're waiting for something to happen, doesn't it? Funny thin is, time can pass very slowly or very fast, and sometimes even both at once. The time now? Oh, a little after four, but what that means should depend on you. Too often, we do something simply because time tells us to. Time for school, time for bed, whoops, 12:00, time to be hungry. It can get a little silly, don't you think? Time is important, but it's what you do with it that makes it so. So my advice to you is to use it. Keep your eyes open and y our ears perked. Otherwise it will pass before you know it, and you'll certainly have missed something!

Things have a h abit of doing that, you know. Being here on minute and gone the next.

In the twinkling of an eye.

In a jiffy.

In a flash!

I know a girl who yawned and missed a whole summer vacation. And what about that caveman who took a nap one afternoon, and woke up to find himself completely alone. You see, while he was sleeping, someone had invented the wheel and everyone had moved to the suburbs. And then of course, there is Milo. *[LIGHTS UP to reveal MILO's Bedroom. The CLOCK appears to be o a shelf in the room of a young boy—a room filled with books, toys, games, maps, papers, pencils, a bed, a desk. There is a dartboard with numbers and the face of the MATHEMEMAGICIAN, a bedspread made from KING AZAZ's cloak, a kite looking like the spelling bee, a punching bag with the HUMBUG's face, as well as records, a television, a toy car, and a large box that is wrapped and has an envelope taped to the top. The sound of FOOTSTEPS is heard, and then enter MILO dejectedly. He throws down his books and coat, flops into a chair, and sighs loudly.]* Who never knows what to do with himself—not just sometimes, but always. When he's in school, he wants to be out, and when he's out, he wants to be in. *[During the following speech, MILO examines the various toys, tools, and other possessions in the room, trying them out and rejecting them.]* Wherever he is, he wants to be somewhere else—and when he gets there, so what. Everything is too much trouble or a waste of time. Books—he's already read them. Games—boring. T.V.—dumb. So what's left? Another long, boring afternoon. Unless he bothers to notice a very large package that happened to arrive today.

MILO. *[Suddenly notices the package. He drags himself over to it, and disinterestedly reads the label.]* "For Milo, who has plenty of time." Well, that's true. *[Sighs and looks at it]*. No. *[Walks away.]* Well…*[Comes back. Rips open envelope and reads.]*

Name ______________________ Date ______________

A VOICE. "one genuine turnpike tollbooth, easily assembled at h ome for use by those who have never traveled in lands beyond.."

MILO. Beyond what? *[Continues reading.]*

A VOICE. "This package contains the following items: " *{MILO pulls the items out of the box and sets them up as they are mentioned.]* "One (1) genuine turnpike tollbooth to be erected according to directions. Three (3) precautionary signs to be used in precautionary fashion. Assorted coins for paying tolls. One (1) map, strictly up to date, showing how to get here to there. One (1) book of rules and traffic regulations which may not be bent or broken. Warning! Results are not guaranteed. If not perfectly satisfied, your wasted time will be refunded."

MILO. *[Skepticall.]* Come off it, who do you think you're *kidding [Walks around and examines tollbooth.]* What am I supposed to do with this? *[The ticking of the CLOCK grows loud and impatient.]* Well…what else do I have to do. *[MILO gets into his toy car and drives up to the first sign.]*

VOICE. "HAVE YOUR DESTINATION IN MIND."

MILO. *[Pulls out the map.]* Now, let's see. That's funny. I never heard of any of these places. Well, it doesn't matter anyway. Dictionopolis. That's a weird name. I might as well go there. *[Begins to move, following map. Drives off.]*

CLOCK. See what I mean? You never know how things are going to get started. But when you're bored, what you need more than anything is a rude awakening.

[The ALARM goes off very loudly as the stage darkens. The sound of the alarm is transformed into the honking of a car horn, and is then joined by the blasts, bleeps, roars and growls of heavy highway traffic. When the lights come up, MILO's bedroom is gone and we see a lonely road in the middle of nowhere.]

Name ______________________________ Date ______________

32. Which of the following lets the reader know that the drama is a fantasy?
- **A.** the boy plays with toys
- **B.** a voice is heard
- **C.** the clock speaks
- **D.** the tollbooth must be assembled

33. What is the main idea of the clock's first lines?
- **A.** Don't sleep your life away.
- **B.** Clocks are very important.
- **C.** Time is important; don't waste it.
- **D.** Clocks are important; don't ignore them.

34. What do the stage directions for Milo's first line show about his character?
- **A.** He is a young boy.
- **B.** He is bored.
- **C.** He is a skeptic.
- **D.** He does not like the clock.

35. Based on the selection, what is the meaning of precautionary?
- **A.** serious
- **B.** warning
- **C.** realistic
- **D.** moving

36. Based on the selection and your understanding of words what is Dictionopolis?
- **A.** a car
- **B.** a place
- **C.** a new character
- **D.** a weird name

37. What *most likely* does the clock mean by "rude awakening"?
- **A.** something that gets your attention
- **B.** a very difficult situation
- **C.** a very loud noise
- **D.** alarming sounds or events

38. Which of the following best describes the clock?
- **A.** a character that understands Milo
- **B.** a character that does not like Milo
- **C.** the most important character in the drama
- **D.** the only fantasy character in the play

39. Which of the following relationships is *most similar* to the relationship below?

Phantom Tollbooth : Dictionopolis
- **A.** grocery store : food
- **B.** school : books
- **C.** school bus : school
- **D.** parents : home

Name ______________________ Date ______________

The Studebaker" by Rick Steber and from Born to the Land by Brent Ashabranner

Read both passages and answer the questions that follow.

Passage 1:

If you had lived in West, Saturday would have been very special. That was the day that the whole family went to town. "If they were lucky they rode in a Studebaker."

From **"The Studebaker"**

by Rick Steber

The Studebaker company made one model of wagon. It was popular out west and easily recognizable with red or yellow running gear and green paint with fancy scrollwork on the wagon box. Over the years the paint weathered and peeled, leaving bare wood that was never repainted.

Many Studebaker wagons were brought over the Oregon Trail and afterward used around the homestead as an all-purpose wagon. When the wagon was not employed as transportation, it was used to carry a variety of rural necessities from water barrels to barbed wire, salt, grain, hay, and lumber.

Homesteaders and farmers in that era were given to fits of wanderlust. After a few years in one location a man might decide to have a look at "new country" and then the Studebaker would be loaded to overflowing with his family's belongings and the team of faithful horses would pull it to the next land of promise.

Passage 2:

In the following passage, Frank, a farmer, is speaking with the author and a photographer about the history of his land and his family while giving them a tour of his farm.

from *Born to the Land: An American Portrait*

by Brent Ashabranner

He showed us some of his equipment. "That tractor cost $18.000 when I bought it in '77," he said, pointing it his International Harvester. "Now it's about $50,000. You can't keep up with that. I buy all my equipment secondhand. There's lots of equipment being auctioned off these days by fellows going out of business."

Frank admits that he keeps his father's tractor partly for sentimental reasons, but he has no such feelings about the 1971 pickup he drives. he keeps it running because it saves him the price of a new one. "I don't need the smell of new paint'" he says.

On the subject of equipment again Frank said, "Years ago all the neighbors around here would throw in and help each other. One would have a thrasher, another bean cutter. But after the war, families became independent and went their separate ways. Now we're reverting to our old ways because we can't afford all equipment need. It's kind of nice."

Name ______________________ Date ______________

40. Based on part 1, the Studebaker was which of the following?
- A. an old car
- B. a wagon used by homesteaders
- C. a car built by Henry Ford
- D. an Oregon wagon

41. Why was the Studebaker easy to recognize?
- A. because of its distinctive colors
- B. because it was old and weathered
- C. because it carried farm products
- D. because it traveled the Oregon trail.

42. Based on the context of part1, what is a *wanderlust*
- A. a wagon
- B. an illness
- C. the need to farm
- D. the desire to travel

43. Why most likely were Studebakers left in the fields?
- A. they were needed near the barn.
- B. the homesteaders had all moved away.
- C. they were old and worn our.
- D. people had started to use motor vehicles.

44. Which of the following best describes Frank in part 2?
- A. A farmer that did not work before the war.
- B. A farmer that does not like his truck.
- C. A farmer that does not like new tools.
- D. A farmer who likes the idea of sharing.

45. Why does Frank buy his equipment second hand?
- A. He is a good mechanic
- B. New equipment is too expensive.
- C. He likes old things.
- D. New equipment cost $18,000

46. Based on the context of part 2, what is a *thrasher*?
- A. a new tractor
- B. an old tractor
- C. farm equipment
- D. old equipment

47. Which of the following relationships is *most similar* to the relationship below?

Frank : farmer
- A. student : teacher
- B. horse : rider
- C. author : writer
- D. novel : book

Name ______________________ Date ______________

Three Views of Irish Immigration

From Out of Ireland by Kerby Miller and Paul Wagner

Under British rule, most farmland in Ireland was used to grow wheat and oats for sale outside of Ireland. Irish peasants depended on the potato for nourishment. Then, in 1845, disease destroyed the potato crop. To escape starvation, thousands of poor Irish families emigrated to the United States. In the first letter below, a young woman in Ireland describes the famine to her parents in Quebec, Canada. The second and third letters were written by new immigrants in New York to their villages back home.

From Social Studies © Prentice-Hall, Inc.

1) Mary Rush:

Ardnaglass, Ireland

September 6, 1846

Mary is writing to her parents to ask for help. She wants to move from Ireland with her husband and children because of the famine.

... We can only say, the scourge of God fell down on Ireland, in taking away the potatoes, they being the only support of the people. So, dear father and mother, if you don't endeavor to take us out of it, it will be the first news you will hear by some friend of me and my little family to be lost by hunger, and there are thousands dread they will share the same fate. So, I conclude with my blessings to you both. . . .For God's sake take us out of poverty, and don't let us die with the hunger.

2) Daniel Guiney:

Buffalo, New York

August 9, 1850

Daniel is writing to his mother and brothers to tell them how he has been received in America by friends and family.

...Dear friends, if you were to see old Denis Danihy, he never was in as good health and looks better than he ever did at home. . . .If you were to see Denis Reen when Daniel Danihy dressed him with clothes suitable for this country, you would think him to be a boss or steward, so that we have scarcely words to state to you how happy we felt at present. And as to the girls that used to be trotting on the bogs at home, to hear them talk English would be of great astonishment to you. Mary Keefe got two dresses, one from Mary Danihy and the other from Biddy Matt.

3) William Dever:

New York, New York

September 14, 1848

William writes to tell his uncle and brothers how the Irish immigrants are treated in New York.

My dear Uncle and Brothers,It's inconceivable the thousands that land here every week from all the old countries flying from tyranny and oppression. Wealthy farmers with their whole families are coming here and purchasing farms, some the best land in the whole world. Germans, French, Hollanders are doing this on a large scale. But most of the Irish come out poor, unable to purchase farms. They work digging quarries, carrying brick and mortar in scorching sun up to the fourth stories of houses, in winter nothing to do, all their money spent. They are despised and kicked about. Many write home they arehappy and wealthy, when they are of that class above mentioned...

Name ______________________ Date ____________

48. What is the main idea of the first letter?
- **A.** A daughter is describing the Irish famine.
- **B.** A daughter is writing about a visit to her parents.
- **C.** A daughter is asking her parents to help her leave Ireland.
- **D.** A daughter is writing to tell her parents she is angry.

49. Based on the context of letter 1, what is the meaning of scourge?
- **A.** islands in distress
- **B.** something that causes crops to fail
- **C.** people in distress
- **D.** something that causes pain and

50. In letter 2, how does Daniel feel about New York and his new life?
- **A.** He is jealous of his cousins.
- **B.** He is happy and glad he emigrated.
- **C.** He is tired and wants to go home.
- **D.** He is happy but needs new clothes.

51. In letter 2, who most likely are Matthew and Denis?
- **A.** old friends or relatives
- **B.** bosses in New York
- **C.** travelers from Ireland
- **D.** son's of Mary Keefe

52. Why *most likely* did Daniel say that Denis looked like a boss when he changed clothes.
- **A.** He was wearing a banker's suit.
- **B.** He acted like he was a New Yorker.
- **C.** The clothes were very nice.
- **D.** The clothes were too big for him.

53. What is the main idea of letter 3?
- **A.** Most Irish immigrants became rich in New York.
- **B.** Most Irish immigrants got very good jobs.
- **C.** Most Irish immigrants were wealthy farmers.
- **D.** Most Irish immigrants were poor and unwanted in New York.

54. Why would most immigrants write home and say they were doing well?
- **A.** They would not want their families to know they were not successful.
- **B.** They wanted other family members to emigrate.
- **C.** They wanted to pretend that they were rich.
- **D.** They were all braggers.

55. Which of the following relationships is most similar to the relationship below?

Irish : British Rule
- **A.** British : America
- **B.** Russia : United states
- **C.** American Indians : Colonist
- **D.** Colonist : India

STOP

Name ______________________ Date ______________

Assessment Practice

Writing Prompts

Prompt 1

You are a teacher. For several weeks you have been noticing that someone has been writing on desks and other pieces of classroom property, but you don't know who it is. You are determined to put a stop to the vandalism in your classroom but you are concerned that a false accusation might alienate your students.

Write a response in which you think of a solution to your problem. Explain what you would do to stop the damage to classroom property.

As you write your response, remember to:

- Focus on the problem that you face, and propose a solution for what to do about the classroom vandalism.
- Consider the purpose, audience, and context of your response.
- Organize your ideas effectively.
- Include specific details that develop your writing.
- Edit your writing for standard grammar and language usage.

Prompt 2

You are out shopping with your best friend at a popular clothing store near your house. As you are getting ready to leave you realize that your friend is preparing to take an item from the rack out of the store without paying for it. Your friend does not know that you have seen the shoplift attempt and you aren't sure what to do.

Write an essay in which you think of a solution to your problem. Explain what you would do if you were confronted with this situation and why.

As you write your essay, remember to:

- Focus on the problem that you face, and propose a solution for what to do about the classroom vandalism.
- Consider the purpose, audience, and context of your essay.
- Organize your ideas effectively.
- Include specific details that develop your writing.
- Edit your writing for standard grammar and language usage.

Name ______________________ Date ______________

ITBS PRACTICE TEST

Vocabulary

DIRECTIONS

This is a test about words and their meanings.

- For each question, you are to decide which one of the four answers has most nearly the same meaning as the underlined word above it.
- Then, on your answer folder, find the row of answer spaces numbered the same as the question. Fill in the answer space that has the same letter as the answer you picked.

The sample on this page shows you what the questions are like and how to mark your answers.

SAMPLE

S1 **To embrace a friend**

A find
B hug
C listen to
D smile at

ANSWER

S1 A **B** C D

Name ______________________ Date ______________

Vocabulary

1 **A <u>clogged</u> drain**

- **A** blocked
- **B** broken
- **C** loose
- **D** rusty

2 **A freshly painted <u>exterior</u>**

- **J** building
- **K** floor
- **L** outside
- **M** trimming

3 **To <u>generate</u> responses**

- **A** display
- **B** interpret
- **C** grade
- **D** produce

4 **A <u>fictional</u> character**

- **J** cruel
- **K** fascinating
- **L** make-believe
- **M** well-known

5 **To <u>highlight</u> questions**

- **A** answer
- **B** ask
- **C** cancel
- **D** stress

6 **A <u>grouchy</u> dog**

- **J** crabby
- **K** curious
- **L** helpless
- **M** watchful

7 **Feeling <u>lightheaded</u>**

- **A** cranky
- **B** dizzy
- **C** happy
- **D** sleepy

8 **To <u>loathe</u> an enemy**

- **J** despise
- **K** put up with
- **L** scare
- **M** talk to

9 **A speedy <u>recovery</u>**

- **A** change
- **B** completion
- **C** healing
- **D** trip

10 **A different <u>aspect</u>**

- **J** feature
- **K** file
- **L** answer
- **M** scene

11 **A loud <u>clamor</u>**

- **A** ballad
- **B** color
- **C** machine
- **D** racket

12 **A <u>bewildering</u> action**

- **J** amusing
- **K** annoying
- **L** horrifying
- **M** puzzling

13 **A humble <u>abode</u>**

- **A** attitude
- **B** home
- **C** letter
- **D** style

14 **To <u>devise</u> a plan**

- **J** come up with
- **K** put into action
- **L** repeat
- **M** take over

Name ______________________ Date ______________

Reading Comprehension

DIRECTIONS

This is a test of how well you understand what you read.

- This test consists of reading passages followed by questions.
- Read each passage and then answer the questions.
- Four answers are given for each question. You are to choose the answer that you think is better than the others.
- Then, on your answer folder, find the row of answer spaces numbered the same as the question. Fill in the answer space for the best answer.

The sample on this page shows you what the questions are like and how to mark your answers.

SAMPLE

As Lisa walked home from school, she thought about Mason and how sad he looked when Ms. Felter told him his science grade. "I should have helped him study," she said out loud. "He would have done that much for me." Lisa remembered all the times Mason had been there for her. When she had fallen off her bike, he had helped her up and brushed her off. When she had forgotten her lunch, he had given her half of his. He was the best friend anyone could ever have.

S1 **How does Lisa feel about Mason's science grade?**

A Angry
B Guilty
C Surprised
D Unconcerned

ANSWER

S1 A **B** C D

Name ______________________ Date ______________

In "Childhood and Poetry," Pablo Neruda describes a memorable event from his youth. He is playing in his yard when a small, unidentified hand reaches through a hole in the fence and places a toy sheep on the ground. Years later, Neruda recalls how this exchange of gifts between strangers helped him give light to his poetry.

¶1 One time, investigating in the backyard of our house in Temuco the tiny objects and minuscule beings of my world, I came upon a hole in one of the boards of the fence. I looked through the hole and saw a landscape like that behind our house, uncared for, and wild. I moved back a few steps, because I sensed vaguely that something was about to happen. All of a sudden a hand appeared—a tiny hand of a boy about my own age. By the time I came close again, the hand was gone, and in its place there was a marvelous white sheep.

¶2 The sheep's wool was faded. Its wheels had escaped. All of this only made it more authentic. I had never seen such a wonderful sheep. I looked back through the hole but the boy had disappeared. I went into the house and brought out a treasure of my own: a pinecone, opened, full of odor and resin, which I adored. I set it down in the same spot and went off with the sheep.

¶3 I never saw either the hand or the boy again. And I have never again seen a sheep like that either. The toy I lost finally in a fire. But even now, in 1954, almost 50 years old, whenever I pass a toy shop, I look furtively into the window, but it's no use. They don't make sheep like that any more.

¶4 I have been a lucky man. To feel the intimacy of brothers is a marvelous thing in life. To feel the love of people whom we love is a fire that feeds our life. But to feel the affection that comes from those whom we do not know, from those unknown to us, who are watching over our sleep and solitude, over our dangers and our weaknesses—that is something still greater and more beautiful because it widens out the boundaries of our being, and unites all living things.

¶5 That exchange brought home to me for the first time a precious idea: that all of humanity is somehow together. That experience came to me again much later; this time it stood out strikingly against a background of trouble and persecution.

¶6 It won't surprise you then that I attempted to give something resiny, earthlike, and fragrant in exchange for human brotherhood. Just as I once left the pinecone by the fence, I have since left my words on the door of so many people who were unknown to me, people in prison, or hunted, or alone.

¶7 That is the great lesson I learned in my childhood, in the backyard of a lonely house. Maybe it was nothing but a game two boys played who didn't know each other and wanted to pass to the other some good things of life. Yet maybe this small and mysterious exchange of gifts remained inside me also, deep and indestructible, giving my poetry light.

Name ______________________ Date ______________

1 Why did the little boy give the author the toy sheep?

A He felt sorry for the author.
B He wanted to be nice to the author.
C The author had given him a pinecone.
D The author had asked him for the sheep.

2 How does the author regard the toy sheep?

J As earthlike
K As intelligent
L As precious
M As threatening

3 In paragraph 6, what does the author mean when he says, "I have since left my words on the door of so many people"?

A Many people have read his poetry.
B He has sent letters to many people.
C He has conversed with many people.
D Many people have seen his drawings.

4 Which of these best describes the author's way of expressing himself?

J He carefully describes an event exactly the way it happened.
K He uses a simple childhood event to illustrate an important idea.
L He uses persuasive language to convince the reader of his opinion.
M He uses unbelievable exaggerations to let the reader know that he is telling a tall tale.

5 The author believes affection from people we don't know

A is usually not welcome.
B keeps us safe from danger.
C unites us with all living things.
D happens only during childhood.

6 In paragraph 7, what does "indestructible" mean?

J Adjustable
K Distinguishable
L Incapable
M Unbreakable

Name ______________________ Date ____________

In this excerpt from the short story "Names/Nombres," Julia Alvarez recalls her family's early years as immigrants to the United States from the Dominican Republic. She describes how her family continually adjusted to the mispronunciation of their names.

¶1 When we arrived in New York City, our names changed almost immediately. At Immigration, the officer asked my father, *Mister Elbures,* if he had anything to declare. My father shook his head, "No," and we were waved through. I was too afraid we wouldn't be let in if I corrected the man's pronunciation, but I said our name to myself, opening my mouth wide for the organ blast of the *a,* trilling my tongue for the drumroll of the *r, All-vah-rrr-es!* How could anyone get *Elbures* out of that orchestra of sound?

¶2 At the hotel my mother was *Missus Alburest,* and I was *little girl,* as in, "Hey little girl, stop riding the elevator up and down. It's *not* a toy."

¶3 When we moved into our new apartment building, the super called my father *Mister Alberase,* and the neighbors who became mother's friends pronounced her name *Jew-lee-ah* instead of *Hoo-lee-ah.* I, her namesake, was known as *Hoo-lee-tah* at home. But at school, I was *Judy* or *Judith,* and once an English teacher mistook me for *Juliet.*

¶4 It took awhile to get used to my new names. I wondered if I shouldn't correct my teachers and new friends. But my mother argued that it didn't matter. "You know what your friend Shakespeare said, *'A rose by any other name would smell as sweet.'*" My father had gotten into the habit of calling any famous author "my friend" because I had begun to write poems and stories in English class.

7 When the people at the hotel called the author "little girl," they were

A giving her a nickname.
B hoping she would speak to them.
C speaking to her in a negative way.
D doing what her mother had told them do.

8 How did the author feel when her classmates called her *Judy* or *Judith*?

J Upset
K Ashamed
L Nervous
M Proud

9 In paragraph 4, what is meant by the quotation "A rose by any other name would smell as sweet"?

A Names are unimportant.
B People can live without names.
C A name is beautiful like a rose.
D The author's name is sweet like a rose.

10 In what way are famous authors Julia's "friends"?

J She is in classes with them at school.
K She reads their stories and poems.
L She also writes stories and poems.
M She is the top student in her English class.

Name ______________________________ Date ______________

In "Abuelito Who," by Sandra Cisneros, the speaker weaves earlier, happier impressions of her grandfather with her impressions of him as a frail man who "sleeps in his little room all night and day."

Abuelito[1] who throws coins like rain
and asks who loves him
who is dough and feathers
who is a watch and glass of water
whose hair is made of fur
is too sad to come downstairs today
who tells me in Spanish you are my diamond
who tells me in English you are my sky
whose little eyes are string
can't come out to play
sleeps in his little room all night and day
who used to laugh like the letter k
is sick
is a doorknob tied to a sour stick
is tired shut the door
doesn't live here anymore
is hiding underneath the bed
who talks to me inside my head
is blankets and spoons and big brown shoes
who snores up and down up and down
up and down again
is the rain on the roof that falls like coins
asking who loves him
who loves him who?

[1]**Abuelito** (ä bwe lē´ tō): In Spanish, an affectionate term for a grandfather.

11 **When the author says her grandfather "talks to me inside my head," she means**

A she is thinking about him.
B he is whispering in her ear.
C she has troubling hearing him.
D her mother is talking about him.

12 **How does the speaker of the poem feel about her grandfather?**

J Angry
K Confused
L Nervous
M Thrilled

13 **What does the speaker mean in the last line of the poem?**

A Her grandfather is in a hospital.
B She does not love her grandfather.
C She has never seen her grandfather.
D She no longer recognizes her grandfather.

14 **When the speaker says her grandfather is "dough and feathers" she means he is**

J large.
K soft.
L thin.
M warm.

Name ______________________ Date ____________

Spelling

DIRECTIONS

This test will show how well you can spell.

- Many of the questions in this test contain mistakes in spelling. Some do not have any mistakes at all.
- You should look for mistakes in spelling.
- When you find a mistake, fill in the answer space on your answer folder that has the same letter as the **line** containing the mistake.
- If there is no mistake, fill in the last answer space.

The samples on this page show you what the questions are like and how to mark your answers.

SAMPLES

S1
A explane
B hornet
C brilliance
D devote
E *(No mistakes)*

S2
J hopeless
K parcel
L radar
M repair
N *(No mistakes)*

ANSWERS

S1 **A** B C D E

S2 J K L M **N**

Name ____________________ Date ____________

Spelling

1 **A** harmful
B greatful
C healthful
D playful
E *(No mistakes)*

2 **J** clamor
K docter
L flounder
M sailor
N *(No mistakes)*

3 **A** hoarse
B cinch
C ought
D drought
E *(No mistakes)*

4 **J** plague
K leegue
L earn
M turn
N *(No mistakes)*

5 **A** impresion
B infection
C reflection
D inscription
E *(No mistakes)*

6 **J** protector
K encountor
L deliver
M producer
N *(No mistakes)*

7 **A** amazement
B element
C improvment
D refreshment
E *(No mistakes)*

8 **J** diagram
K absolute
L buttermilk
M canary
N *(No mistakes)*

9 **A** deliteful
B forgetful
C regretful
D plentiful
E *(No mistakes)*

10 **J** gourmet
K bouquet
L context
M afflict
N *(No mistakes)*

11 **A** detergent
B principal
C accomplis
D computer
E *(No mistakes)*

12 **J** dwarf
K moose
L ounce
M raise
N *(No mistakes)*

13 **A** reaction
B election
C collection
D atraction
E *(No mistakes)*

14 **J** feilder
K welder
L flutter
M glitter
N *(No mistakes)*

Name ______________________ Date ______________

Capitalization

DIRECTIONS

This is a test on capitalization. It will show how well you can use capital letters in sentences.

- You should look for mistakes in capitalization in the sentences on this test.
- When you find a mistake, fill in the answer space on your answer folder that has the same letter as the **line** containing the mistake.
- Some sentences do not have any mistakes at all. If there is no mistake, fill in the last answer space.

The samples on this page show you what the questions are like and how to mark your answers.

SAMPLES

S1 **A** Anne Tyler, the author
B of *Breathing lessons,* is one
C of my all-time favorite writers.
D *(No mistakes)*

S2 **J** Kristina's father bought
K her a new blue Convertible
L for her sixteenth birthday.
M *(No mistakes)*

S3 **A** If you ever visit Norway, be
B sure to see the ancient ships
C kept in the museums.
D *(No mistakes)*

ANSWERS

S1 A **B** C D
S2 J **K** L M
S3 A B C **D**

Name ______________________________ Date ______________

Capitalization

1 **A** My teacher rolled his eyes
B and said, "please don't tell me
C the dog ate your homework."
D *(No mistakes)*

2 **J** A Tanager is a beautiful, colorful
K bird that is very common in the
L Southwest and in southern California.
M *(No mistakes)*

3 **A** "Would you be kind enough to carry
B this great big suitcase for me?" the sweet
C old woman asked the worried little boy.
D *(No mistakes)*

4 **J** Last winter we visited aunt Carrie
K in Mesa, Arizona, where
L she owns a small summer home.
M *(No mistakes)*

5 **A** *The Horse whisperer,* a novel by
B Nicholas Evans, about a man who talks
C to horses, is set in Montana.
D *(No mistakes)*

6 **J** Jamie lives West of our
K house, on Hamilton Street, in
L a town called Wyoming.
M *(No mistakes)*

7 **A** In the late 1800s, the Brontë
B Sisters published novels under the
C names Currier, Ellis, and Acton Bell.
D *(No mistakes)*

8 **J** 155 Hightop Drive, Apt. 4
K Binghamton, NY
L September 27, 2001
M *(No mistakes)*

9 **A** Dr. Carol Harris
B Riverview college
C Dear Dr. Harris:
D *(No mistakes)*

10 **J** I am writing this letter to tell you how
K much I enjoyed your book, *Planetary Wonders.*
L I particularly enjoyed the chapter about mars.
M *(No mistakes)*

11 **A** I would also like to ask you if I may
B photocopy chapter 9 for an oral presentation
C I am giving on the solar system.
D *(No mistakes)*

12 **J** I'm in the sixth grade at Montgomery Elementary.
K Sincerely yours,
L Charles Moyerowski
M *(No mistakes)*

13 **A** My sister Cara is a successful
B photographer who worked her way
C through College and supported me as well.
D *(No mistakes)*

Name ______________________________ Date ______________

Punctuation

DIRECTIONS

This is a test on punctuation. It will show how well you can use periods, question marks, commas, and other kinds of punctuation marks.

- You should look for mistakes in punctuation in the sentences on this test.
- When you find a mistake, fill in the answer space on your answer folder that has the same letter as the **line** containing the mistake.
- Some sentences do not have any mistakes at all. If there is no mistake, fill in the last answer space.

The samples on this page show you what the questions are like and how to mark your answers.

SAMPLES

S1
A The three girls earned the
B money for the trip by baby-sitting
C and saving their allowances.
D *(No mistakes)*

S2
J Because of the upcoming
K snowstorm school was
L dismissed at noon today.
M *(No mistakes)*

S3
A The dog liked three things
B best, running in the field,
C chasing the ball, and eating.
D *(No mistakes)*

ANSWERS

S1 A B C **D**

S2 J **K** L M

S3 A **B** C D

Name ______________________ Date ______________

Punctuation

1 **A** The Norway Spruce an evergreen
B tree, was brought to the United
C States from Europe.
D *(No mistakes)*

2 **J** On December 10 1949 the
K AAFC and NFL merged and made
L the Cleveland Browns part of the NFL.
M *(No mistakes)*

3 **A** Sara knew her little sister wasn't telling
B the truth because she rolled her eyes and
C said "Give me a break already, will you?"
D *(No mistakes)*

4 **J** Even though Arthur Harris earned straight
K A's since the first grade, each time he took a
L test he asked the teacher, "How did I do."
M *(No mistakes)*

5 **A** My 71-year-old mother writes novels,
B paints pictures, sings in the
C choir, and is a devout baseball fan.
D *(No mistakes)*

6 **J** The clavicle is a long thin bone
K located at the root of the neck. Just below
L the skin in front of the first rib.
M *(No mistakes)*

7 **A** Michelangelo who spent his life
B in Florence and Rome, was a talented
C painter, sculptor, poet, and architect.
D *(No mistakes)*

8 **J** Brackton Middle School
K Brackton, PA 18641
L January 10 2000
M *(No mistakes)*

9 **A** Dear Friend:
B The students at Brackton Area Middle School are
C holding the annual Valentine's Day dance on February 14.
D *(No mistakes)*

10 **J** Would you consider donating party supplies
K for the dance. The proceeds from ticket sales
L to the dance will benefit local charities.
M *(No mistakes)*

11 **A** Thank you for your consideration.
B Sincerely,
C The Students at Brackton Middle School
D *(No mistakes)*

12 **J** Because of rising airline costs
K many people are choosing to drive
L to vacation spots instead of flying.
M *(No mistakes)*

Name ______________________________ Date ______________

Usage and Expression

DIRECTIONS

This is a test on the use of words. It will show how well you can use words according to the standards of correctly written English.

- You should look for mistakes in the sentences on this test.
- When you find a mistake, fill in the answer space on your answer folder that has the same letter as the **line** containing the mistake.
- Some sentences do not have any mistakes at all. If there is no mistake, fill in the last answer space.

The samples on this page show you what the questions are like and how to mark your answers.

SAMPLES

S1
A When it comes to science, both of
B my favorite teachers, Mrs. Keton and
C Ms. Connelly, knows her stuff.
D *(No mistakes)*

S2
J Ernest Hemingway was a
K famous writer who living in a mansion
L in Key West with over 60 cats.
M *(No mistakes)*

ANSWERS

S1 A B **C** D

S2 J **K** L M

Name ______________________ Date ____________

Usage

1 **A** Each of the girls knows the
B combination to their locker as well
C as her identification number.
D *(No mistakes)*

2 **J** Stephen King, a famous horror
K writer, usually writing his novels in
L the basement of his home.
M *(No mistakes)*

3 **A** Shelby said she don't have no idea
B why her brother didn't show up for
C band practice last Tuesday.
D *(No mistakes)*

4 **J** A cat named Shade McCorkle
K once saved his owner's life
L by fending off an intruder.
M *(No mistakes)*

5 **A** Most physicians agree that, in
B addition to improving your muscle
C tone, exercise can lifting your spirits.
D *(No mistakes)*

6 **J** Some people believe that e-mail will
K eventually replace mail as the primary
L means of written correspondence.
M *(No mistakes)*

7 **A** After scuba diving for three
B days, we found the rare puffer fish,
C just what we was looking for.
D *(No mistakes)*

8 **J** A recent survey showed that many
K Americans don't realize that 220
L is a high cholesterol level.
M *(No mistakes)*

9 **A** My mother's store of
B patience is great, but my father's
C is even more greater.
D *(No mistakes)*

10 **J** For all their power, the human
K heart is amazingly small—about
L the size of two fists.
M *(No mistakes)*

Name ______________________________ Date ______________

Expression

DIRECTIONS

This is Part 2 of the test about the use of words. It will show how well you can express ideas correctly and effectively. There are several sections to this part of the test. Read the directions to each section carefully. Then mark your answers on your answer folder.

Directions: Use this paragraph to answer questions 11–14.

[1]The *Tyrannosaurus Rex,* or T-Rex as it is commonly called, was a gigantic dinosaur that roamed North America more than 70 million years ago. [2]Its head was more than 4 feet long, and some of its teeth were larger than a human hand. [3]T-Rex stood about 19 feet high and was <u>pretty close to</u> 47 feet long. [4]Its massive tail was probably used to balance its heavy head. [5]Dimetrodon was the most common meat-eating dinosaur and lived in Permian times, almost 260 million years ago.

11 Which is the best place for sentence 2?

- **A** Where it is now
- **B** Before Sentence 1
- **C** Between Sentences 3 and 4
- **D** After Sentence 5

12 Which sentence should be left out of this paragraph?

- **J** Sentence 1
- **K** Sentence 2
- **L** Sentence 4
- **M** Sentence 5

13 Which is the best way to rewrite the underlined part of sentence 3?

- **A** about
- **B** probably almost
- **C** somewhere around
- **D** *(No change)*

14 Which is the best concluding sentence for this paragraph?

- **J** Scientists are still unsure what happened to T-Rex that made it become extinct.
- **K** Although the T-Rex was massive, it was not as feared as the Velociraptor, a smaller dinosaur that hunted in packs.
- **L** The T-Rex has been featured in many movies, some of them enormously popular.
- **M** Scientists believe T-Rex mothers were extremely protective of their young.

Name ______________________________ Date ______________

Directions: In questions 15–16, choose the best way to express the idea.

15
- **A** Many experts believe that a fear of public speaking can be conquered with practice.
- **B** With practice, a fear of public speaking can be conquered, many experts believe.
- **C** A belief held by many experts is that a fear of public speaking can be conquered with practice.
- **D** That a fear of public speaking can be conquered with a practice, is a belief held by many experts.

16
- **J** The gray squirrel is common in the North, but frequently raids bird feeders and garbage cans.
- **K** The gray squirrel, which is common in the North, frequently raids bird feeders and garbage cans.
- **L** While the gray squirrel is common in the North, it frequently raids bird feeders and garbage cans.
- **M** A frequent raider of bird feeders and garbage cans is the gray squirrel that's common in the North.

Directions: In questions 17–19, choose the best way to write the underlined part of the sentence.

17 My little sister Kelsy likes to sing, <u>dancing</u>, and play the piano.

A will dance **B** dance **C** to dance **D** *(No change)*

18 I should <u>have went</u> to the game, instead of just watching television all evening.

J have gone **K** had went **L** going **M** *(No change)*

---

19 **Which of these would be most persuasive in a letter to the school board?**

- **A** We students feel the new mandatory community service requirement for all graduating seniors is unfair. Many of us have after-school jobs and can't spare 10 hours a month. In addition, some of our parents can't provide us with the necessary transportation to and from the service facility we are assigned.
- **B** Some of us seniors don't like the new mandatory community service requirement. Making us serve the community in order to graduate isn't fair. We want to spend our time in other ways. How can we find time to study and serve the community? Please reconsider this requirement.
- **C** We're attending this meeting to try to persuade you to change the new mandatory community service requirement. You're forcing us to do something we may not want to do.
- **D** The new community service requirement is completely unfair. Seniors don't want to do this. We need to spend time with our friends. We have a petition with us. Basically, we refuse to do this.

Name ______________________ Date ______________

TERRANOVA PRACTICE TEST

Reading and Language Arts

Sample Passage

Respect

People from various cultures have different ways of showing respect toward one another. In some cultures people shake hands upon meeting. In others, people hug each other as a way of greeting. In the United States, eye contact is encouraged, but in some cultures, eye contact is a sign of rudeness.

Sample A

This passage is mostly about

Ⓐ how people show respect

Ⓑ how people shake hands

Ⓒ why eye contact is rude

Ⓓ why greetings are important

Name ______________________ Date ______________

Directions

A student wrote a paragraph about his older brother. There are some mistakes that need correcting.

[1]For as long as I can remember, my older brother Mark has been there. [2]Mark has always been there for me. [3]He taught me how to have faith in myself and to stand up for what I believe in. [4]I always knew that whenever I had a problem, Mark would be there for me, trying to make things better.

Sample B

Which of these best combines Sentences 1 and 2?

Ⓕ For as long as I can remember, my older brother Mark has been there for me.

Ⓖ My older brother Mark, for as long as I can remember, has been there for me.

Ⓗ Because my older brother Mark has been there, for as long as I can remember.

Ⓙ My older brother Mark has always been there for me, at least as long as I can remember.

Sample C

Where would this sentence best fit into the paragraph?

I know he'll also be there for me in the future.

Ⓐ after Sentence 1

Ⓑ after Sentence 2

Ⓒ after Sentence 3

Ⓓ after Sentence 4

Name ______________________________ Date ______________

Far-Away Places

Have you ever visited a far-away place? Many people travel to different places on vacations or to visit friends and family. Visiting someplace that's very different from your home can be a great learning experience—and a lot of fun.

In this theme you'll read about some people who have visited some fascinating places, and you'll have a chance to write about a place you would like to visit. Start Reading and begin learning about **Far-Away Places.**

The Loch Ness Monster *by* George Laycock

Directions

Each year, tourists flock to Loch Ness, Scotland, in the hopes of catching a glimpse of Nessie, the famous Loch Ness monster. While many doubt that the monster actually exists, in this excerpt from "The Loch Ness Monster," George Laycock discusses why researchers are beginning to believe that Nessie may be real after all. Read the excerpt. Then, do Numbers 1 through 6.

In 1938, a tugboat captain was steering his boat across Loch Ness. Everything seemed to be in order. The sky was cloudy just as it is much of the time around Loch Ness. The water was rough from the wind. The tug plowed on mile after mile, its engines laboring normally. The captain was not thinking about monsters. He didn't believe in Nessie anyhow. He made this plain enough to anyone who asked him if he'd ever seen the beast. Then beside the boat, a creature like nothing the captain had ever seen before stuck its long humped back out of the water. It had a long, slender neck and a little head. The monster rushed ahead, gained speed on the tug, and disappeared far out in front of the boat. This was enough to change the captain's mind. As far as he was concerned, Nessie was real, after all.

Other sightings even included an observation by a driver who saw Nessie in the beam of his headlights on a dark night as the monster crossed the highway near the loch.

These stories were told and retold. Word of Nessie spread around the world. This did a marvelous thing for Scotland. Tourists began to visit Loch Ness, hoping for a glimpse of the elusive lake monster. Tourism can be good for a country's economy. Nessie, real or not, became the most valuable animal in all Scotland.

But the lecturer who was to tell us about the Loch Ness monster that night in Oxford, Ohio, had brought scientific methods to the search for Nessie, and people were eager to hear his message. All the seats were filled and students stood around the walls and sat in the aisles to listen to the story Robert H. Rines had to tell.

Dr. Rines, president of the Boston Academy of Applied Science, led his first scientific expedition to Loch Ness in 1970. He took along modern sonar equipment and used this to "see" into the murky depths. Sonar works by sending high-intensity sound impulses into the water and measuring the echoes sent back as the sound waves bounce off the bottom or off objects between it and the bottom. It can reveal the depth of objects in the water, their size, and whether or not they are moving. That summer the sonar equipment showed the researchers important facts. There were large moving objects in the loch. Also there were abundant fish to feed monsters.

Dr. Rines meanwhile was consulting with his colleagues, searching for still better equipment for gathering information about the monster of Loch Ness. He worked with Dr. Harold E. Edgerton, who, as a professor at Massachusetts Institute of Technology, had pioneered in the development of high-speed underwater photography. Dr. Edgerton had also developed remarkable strobe lights for making pictures in dingy water. Now, he designed a system of lights Dr. Rines might use to obtain closeup pictures in Loch Ness.

Dr. Rines linked his camera to the sonar and set it so that it would begin making pictures automatically as soon as any large object passed through the sonar field. It would continue to make pictures every fifteen seconds as long as the sonar told it to.

For their first test, the crew of monster seekers chose the bay where Nessie had most often been sighted. They carefully cleaned the camera lens, then began lowering it gently toward the lake bottom. Divers checked it there and found it clean and ready to make monster pictures.

Another camera was suspended under the research boat and pointed downward into the dark water. All that was needed now was to wait for Nessie to come nosing around.

But a strange thing happened. The lens of the camera on the bottom of the loch was suddenly covered with sand, apparently kicked onto it by some large frightened creature. Had Nessie been there and kicked up the silt?

That camera, with its sand-covered lens, made no pictures. But the other camera, hanging beneath the boat, was still in working order. It yielded pictures that to some looked plainly like parts of a huge unknown monster swimming in the water. These color pictures were perhaps the best evidence that there really is a Nessie.

1 Choose the sentence that best describes what the passage is mostly about.

Ⓐ The Loch Ness monster may actually be a large water reptile.

Ⓑ New evidence is convincing more people that the Loch Ness monster is real.

Ⓒ A tugboat captain recounts seeing the Loch Ness monster swim past his boat.

Ⓓ Some scientists refuse to believe in the Loch Ness monster, in spite of evidence that it may be real.

2 According to the passage, while Dr. Rines was using sonar to "see" the depths of the Loch, he was also "consulting with his colleagues, searching for still better equipment." The word *colleagues* probably means

Ⓕ employees

Ⓖ neighbors

Ⓗ peers

Ⓙ supplies

3 Which of these best describes Dr. Rines?

Ⓐ content

Ⓑ disappointed

Ⓒ nervous

Ⓓ hopeful

Name ______________________________ Date ______________

4 The answer you chose for Number 3 is best because you learned from the passage that

Ⓕ Dr. Rines was unable to prove that the monster exists.

Ⓖ Dr. Rines gathered evidence that may prove the monster is real.

Ⓗ Dr. Rines was worried that the monster would damage his sonar equipment.

Ⓙ Dr. Rines believed that he had gathered enough evidence to prove that the monster is real.

5 Stories of the Loch Ness monster were good for Scotland because

Ⓐ scientists visited the loch to gather research

Ⓑ students visited the loch to study the monster

Ⓒ tourists visited the loch hoping to see the monster

Ⓓ fisherman visited the loch hoping to catch the monster

6 In the passage, the author says that people "began to visit Loch Ness, hoping for a glimpse of the elusive lake monster." The word *elusive* probably means

Ⓕ aggressive

Ⓖ huge

Ⓗ shy

Ⓙ strange

Name ______________________________ Date ______________

Directions

Ms. Chan's class is writing about places they have visited or places they would like to visit. Carol wrote about a visit to see her aunt and uncle in Ocean City, Maryland. Here is her essay. There are several mistakes that need correcting.

[1]Last summer, my Aunt Deeny and Uncle Phil invited my brother Marc and me to spend two weeks with them at their home in Ocean City, Maryland. [2]Marc and I live in Ohio, we had never been to the ocean, so we were very excited. [3]Aunt Deeny and Uncle Phil live in a house that's next to a beautiful bay. [4]They have a dock in the back of the house, so they can driving their boat right up to their back door. [5]Marc and I spent most of our days at the beach, which is beautiful. [6]The beach is very crowded in the summer. [7]Uncle Phil taught Marc and I to learn how to bodyboard. [8]You put the bodyboard underneath your stomach and glide on the waves. [9]We weren't very good at it when we first tried it. [10]I scraped my arms and swallowed some sea water. [11]However, by the end of the trip, we was very good. [12]Even though the beach was a blast, the best part of the trip was spending time with Aunt Deeny and Uncle Phil. [13]I hope we can visit them again next summer.

7 Which sentence contains two complete thoughts and should be written as two sentences?

Ⓐ Sentence 1

Ⓑ Sentence 2

Ⓒ Sentence 11

Ⓓ Sentence 12

8 The best way to write Sentence 4 is

Ⓕ In the back of their house, they have a dock so they drive their boat right up to the back.

Ⓖ They have a dock in the back of the house, so they can drive their boat right up to their back door.

Ⓗ They will drive their boat right up to the back door, because they have a dock in the back of the house.

Ⓙ Best as it is

Name ______________________ Date ______________

9 Which of these best combines Sentences 5 and 6?

Ⓐ Marc and I spent most of our days at the beach, which is beautiful and very crowded in the summer.

Ⓑ Marc and I spent most of our days at the beautiful beach, which is also very crowded in the summer.

Ⓒ The beach is beautiful in the summer and very crowded, but Marc and I spent most of our days there.

Ⓓ The beach is very crowded in the summer and Marc and I spent most of our days at the beach, which is beautiful.

10 Which is the best way to write Sentence 7?

Ⓕ Uncle Phil taught Marc and me how to bodyboard.

Ⓖ Marc and I were taught by Uncle Phil how to bodyboard.

Ⓗ Marc and I learned how to bodyboard from Uncle Phil, who taught us.

Ⓙ Best as it is

11 Choose the best way to write Sentence 11.

Ⓐ We was very good by the end of the trip, however.

Ⓑ When the trip ended, we were very good, however.

Ⓒ However, by the end of the trip, we were very good.

Ⓓ Best as it is

12 Where would this sentence best fit in the paragraph?

A bodyboard looks like a small surfboard.

Ⓕ after Sentence 7

Ⓖ after Sentence 8

Ⓗ after Sentence 9

Ⓙ after Sentence 10

Name ______________________ Date ______________

An Astronaut's Answers *by* John Glenn

Directions

In this interview, John Glenn answers questions about what it's like to travel in space. John Glenn was the first American to travel around the Earth in space, on February 20, 1962. He orbited the Earth three times in the spacecraft *Friendship 7*. Thirty-six years later at age 77, on board the shuttle *Discovery*, he became the oldest person ever to travel in space. Read the interview. Then, do numbers 13 to 18.

The first time you went into space, how did it feel to be all alone except for communication through radio?

In 1962, I looked down from an orbit high above our planet and saw our beautiful Earth and its curved horizon against the vastness of space. I have never forgotten that sight nor the sense of wonder it engendered. Although I was alone in *Friendship 7*, I did not feel alone in space. I knew that I was supported by my family, my six fellow astronauts, thousands of NASA engineers and employees, and millions of people around the world.

Why did you want to be an astronaut? How did you fly around the Earth three times? Was it hard?

I served as a fighter pilot in World War II and the Korean conflict. After Korea, I graduated from the Naval Test Pilot School and worked as a fighter test pilot. I applied for the astronaut program because I thought it was a logical career step, a challenging opportunity and one in which I could help start a new area of research that would be very valuable to everyone here and on Earth. I have always considered myself very fortunate to be selected in the first group of seven astronauts.

An Atlas rocket boosted me into space and I orbited the Earth in my space capsule, the *Friendship 7*. It certainly was a challenge but one for which I was well prepared. The National Aeronautics and Space Administration (NASA) wanted people who were test pilots and accustomed to working under very unusual conditions, including emergencies. During my first orbit, I experienced some troubles with the automatic control system and so I had to take control of the capsule's movements by hand for the rest of the trip. Another problem developed when the signals showed that the head shield was loose. To keep it secured during re-entry, I kept the retrorocket pack in place to steady the shield. When the *Friendship 7* entered the atmosphere, the retrorocket pack burned off and flew by the window, but the head shield stayed in place. These were problems we could not have foreseen prior to the flight.

How long was your trip around the Earth?

My trip around the Earth lasted 4 hours and 55 minutes, and I flew about 81,000 miles.

What did you eat while you were in outer space?

I took along a number of different kinds of food, such as applesauce and a mixture of meat and vegetables, all emulsified like baby food. It was packaged in containers much like toothpaste tubes so I could squeeze food into my mouth. I had no trouble eating any of it and it tasted fine.

Why do astronauts go to the moon?

As adventurers of earlier eras crossed oceans and scaled mountains, astronauts in our time have flown to the moon and explored the heavens. The crucial hands-on experience of my flight in the Mercury program helped make the Gemini flights possible. The Gemini flights then helped make the Apollo missions to the moon a reality. Apollo gave us valuable information for the Shuttle missions, and the Shuttle/Mir program prepares us for the International

Space Station. This is the nature of progress. Each of the missions has built on the knowledge gained from the previous flights.

We are a curious, questing people and our research in this new laboratory of space represents an opportunity to benefit people right here on Earth and to increase our understanding of the universe. The potential scientific, medical, and economic benefits from space are beyond our wildest dreams. That's why astronauts went to the moon, and that's why we continue to pursue our dreams of space exploration.

13 **The interview you have just read is mostly about**

- Ⓐ an astronaut's thoughts on space travel
- Ⓑ an astronaut's eating habits
- Ⓒ how people train to become astronauts
- Ⓓ how astronauts survive in spacecraft

14 **John Glenn trained to become an astronaut by**

- Ⓕ building spacecraft
- Ⓖ studying space in college
- Ⓗ working as a fighter pilot
- Ⓙ working as a NASA engineer

15 **According to the interview, why do astronauts travel to the moon?**

- Ⓐ to gain knowledge
- Ⓑ to cross the oceans
- Ⓒ to prepare for the future
- Ⓓ to prove that it can be done

16 **Which of these was probably the hardest part of John Glenn's first time around the earth?**

- Ⓕ being alone
- Ⓖ eating food in tubes
- Ⓗ surviving bad weather conditions
- Ⓙ dealing with mechanical difficulties

17 **The author's purpose for writing this article was probably to report on John Glenn's**

- Ⓐ experiences in space
- Ⓑ dreams for the future
- Ⓒ discoveries of unknown lands
- Ⓓ beliefs about the space program

Name ______________________________ Date ______________

18 Here are two sentences related to the passage.

John Glenn traveled in space aboard the space shuttle Discovery. *He was 77 years old.*

Which of these best combines the two sentences into one?

- Ⓕ He was 77 years old, but John Glenn traveled in space aboard the space shuttle *Discovery.*
- Ⓖ When he was 77 years old, John Glenn traveled in space aboard the space shuttle *Discovery.*
- Ⓗ While John Glenn traveled in space aboard the space shuttle *Discovery,* he was 77 years old.
- Ⓙ John Glenn traveled in space aboard the space shuttle *Discovery,* and he was 77 years old.

Name ______________________ Date ______________

Let's Write

Sample D

There are four mistakes in this paragraph. Let's correct them together.

Last winter, my friend Clara asking me to go on a three-day skiing trip with her. It sounded like fun, but skiing is more harder than you would think. I couldn't even stand the first day. I fell off the ski lift. I felled all the way down the bunny slope. I lost one of my poles in the Woods. I crashed into a fence. Eventually, however, I got the hang of it. I'm still not a great skier, but I have mastered the bunny slope.

19 **A student wrote this paragraph about imaginary trips he takes while camping outdoors with his brother. There are five mistakes in the paragraph. Draw a line through each part that has a mistake, and write the correction above it.**

In the summer my older brother Matt and me sleep in a tent in our backyard. Sometimes we pretending the tent is a space ship that takes us to all kinds of places. Every now and then, we go to the moon in our space ship, although once I fell in a crater and hurted my knee. Other times, we travel from star to star in the ship, and sometimes we stop at a planet to get a bite to eat. Matt can even make our space ship travel back in time, once we pretended we were Cowboys riding our horses across the Great Plains. We never know quite where we'll end up.

Name ______________________________ Date ______________

Directions

Study this poster encouraging students to attend a ski trip.

> **The Middle View Area Ski Club will hold a**
>
> **Ski Trip to Camelback Ski Resort**
>
> **on January 10**
>
> Students, friends, and family of all ages welcome!
>
> Bus leaves the school at 8:30 A.M. and returns at 10:30 P.M.
>
> Cost is $45 a person, including ski rental, lunch, and dinner.
>
> Tickets available at the school office.
>
> ---
>
> The Ski Club needs your help! Students and parents need to organize and supervise the trip.
>
> Call Tony Parks at 555-234-8897 for more information.

20 **Now use the information from the poster to do the following:**

Write the information that is most important if you plan to attend the ski trip.

____

Write the information that is most important if you want to help with the trip.

____

Write one phrase from the poster that is meant to persuade you to help.

____

Name ______________________________ Date ______________

21 **Look back at the excerpt from "The Loch Ness Monster." Now think about John Glenn's experience in outer space. If you could travel to any place in the universe, where would you go and why? What would you do on your trip? Write a paragraph discussing your answer.**

For this answer, be sure to use complete sentences and check your work for correct spelling, capitalization, and punctuation.

Name ______________________________ Date ______________

SAT 10 PRACTICE TEST

Vocabulary

Directions:

Look at each underlined word. Choose the word that means about the same thing.

1 To <u>supervise</u> is to—

A lose

B win

C argue

D oversee

2 Something that is <u>vacant</u> is—

F noisy

G empty

H round

J nearby

3 <u>Mobility</u> refers to—

A motion

B speed

C distance

D height

4 <u>Accurately</u> means—

F purposely

G correctly

H quickly

J recently

Directions:

Read each boxed sentence. Then, read the sentences that follow. Choose the sentence that uses the underlined word in the same way as in the box.

5

<u>Kick</u> the ball into the goal.

In which sentence does the word <u>kick</u> mean the same thing as in the sentence above?

A Janet got a <u>kick</u> out of the comedy show.

B Please don't <u>kick</u> me out of the club.

C Barney should <u>kick</u> the habit of oversleeping.

D It is mean to <u>kick</u> other people.

6

The tree branches <u>shake</u>.

In which sentence does the word <u>shake</u> mean the same thing as in the sentence above?

F Boris drank a chocolate milk <u>shake</u>.

G His hand<u>shake</u> was very strong.

H I can't <u>shake</u> the cold I've had all week.

J The baby likes to <u>shake</u> the rattle.

Name ______________________________ Date ______________

Reading Comprehension

from "Names/Nombres" by Julia Alvarez

Directions:

Read this excerpt from "Names/Nombres" by Julia Alvarez. Then, complete numbers 1 through 4 by choosing the best answer.

When we arrived in New York City, our names changed almost immediately. At Immigration, the officer asked my father, *Mister Elbures*, if he had anything to declare. My father shook his head, "No," and we were waved through. I was too afraid we wouldn't be let in if I corrected the man's pronunciation, but I said our name to myself, opening my mouth wide for the organ blast of the *a*, trilling my tongue for the drum-roll of the *r*, *All-vah-rrr-es!* How could anyone get *Elbures* out of that orchestra of sound?

At the hotel my mother was *Missus Alburest*, and I was little girl, as in, "Hey *little girl*, stop riding the elevator up and down. It's *not* a toy."

When we moved into our new apartment building, the super [the apartment manager] called my father *Mister Alberase*, and the neighbors who became mother's friends pronounced her name *Jew-lee-ah* instead of *Hoo-lee-ah*. I, her namesake, was known as *Hoo-lee-tah* at home. But at school, I was *Judy* or *Judith*, and once an English teacher mistook me for *Juliet*.

It took awhile to get used to my new names. I wondered if I shouldn't correct my teachers and new friends. But my mother argued that it didn't matter. "You know what your friend Shakespeare said, *'A rose by any other name would smell as sweet.'* " My father had gotten into the habit of calling any famous author "my friend" because I had begun to write poems and stories in English class.

1 Why was the author called by so many different names?

A Americans had trouble saying her name.

B She changed her name often in school.

C Her teachers frequently mispronounced her name.

D Her parents called her by different names.

2 The author's mother quotes Shakespeare: "A rose by any other name would smell as sweet." What does she mean by this?

F Names can be confusing.

G Names should appeal to the senses.

H It is silly to give names to people and things.

J A person or thing's name is unimportant.

3 The major conflict in this selection occurs mainly because of—

A differences in cultures

B differences in religion

C differences between family members

D differences between generations

4 Which is the literary point of view in this passage?

F A third-person narrator describes the thoughts of several other people.

G A first-person narrator describes her own thoughts and actions.

H A third-person narrator describes the actions but not the thoughts of others.

J A first-person narrator describes all the thoughts and actions of others.

Name ______________________________ Date ______________

Reading Comprehension

from "Hard as Nails" by Russell Baker

Directions:

Here is an excerpt from *Hard as Nails* by Russell Baker. This essay describes Baker's first job—delivering newspapers in Baltimore. Read this excerpt. Then, complete numbers 5 and 6 by choosing the best answer.

As we walked back to the house she [Baker's mother] said I couldn't have a paper route until I was twelve. And all because of some foolish rule they had down here in Baltimore. You'd think if a boy wanted to work they would encourage him instead of making him stay idle so long that laziness got embedded in his bones.

That was April. We had barely finished the birthday cake in August before Deems came by the apartment and gave me the tools of the newspaper trade: an account book for keeping track of the customers' bills and a long, brown web belt. Slung around one shoulder and across the chest, the belt made it easy to balance fifteen or twenty pounds of papers against the hip. I had to buy my own wire cutters for opening the newspaper bundles the trucks dropped at Wisengoff's store on the corner of Stricker and West Lombard streets.

In February my mother had moved us down from New Jersey, where we had been living with her brother Allen ever since my father died in 1930. This move of hers to Baltimore was a step toward fulfilling a dream. More than almost anything else in the world, she wanted "a home of our own." I'd heard her talk of that "home of our own" all through those endless Depression years when we lived as poor relatives dependent on Uncle Allen's goodness. "A home of our own. One of these days, Buddy, we'll have a home of our own."

That winter she had finally saved just enough to make her move, and she came to Baltimore. There were several reasons for Baltimore. For one, there were people she knew in Baltimore, people she could go to if things got desperate. And desperation was possible, because the moving would exhaust her savings, and the apartment rent was twenty-four dollars a month. She would have to find a job quickly. My sister Doris was only nine, but I was old enough for an after-school job that could bring home a few dollars a week. So as soon as it was legal I went into newspaper work.

5 The author and his family moved to Baltimore because—

A his mother thought the rent was lower in Baltimore.

B his mother wanted them to be near Doris.

C his mother wanted them to have their own home.

D his mother found a job in Baltimore.

6 The author probably wrote this passage to—

F persuade children to get after-school jobs

G show readers the unfairness of child labor

H explain what it is like to live in Baltimore

J entertain readers with a memory from his youth

Name ______________________ Date ______________

Reading Comprehension

from *Talent* by Annie Dillard

Directions:

Read this excerpt from *Talent* by Annie Dillard. Then, complete numbers 7 and 8 by choosing the best answer.

There is no such thing as talent. If there are any inborn, God-given gifts, they are in the precocious fields of music, mathematics, and chess; if you have such a gift, you know it by now. All the rest of us, in all the other fields, are not talented. We all start out dull and weary and uninspired. Apart from a few like Mozart, there never have been any great and accomplished little children in the world. Genius is the product of education.

Perhaps it's a cruel thing to insist that there is no such thing as talent. We all want to believe—at least I do—that being selfless was "easy" for Albert Schweitzer, that Faulkner's novels just popped into his head, that Rembrandt painted because he "had to." We want to believe all these nonsensical things in order to get ourselves off the hook. For if these people had no talent, then might the rest of us have painting or writing or great thinking as an option? We, who have no talent? I think the answer is yes, absolutely.

7 What is the major purpose of this selection?

A to make a point about talent

B to persuade people to write novels

C to entertain with a story about talent

D to show why people are afraid of success

8 What does the writer mean when she says, "There is no such thing as talent"?

F People are rarely good at things.

G Nobody works hard anymore.

H People achieve great things through hard work.

J Nobody does things that are truly worthwhile.

Name ______________________________ Date ______________

Reading Comprehension

from "Becky and the Wheels-and-Brake Boys" by James Berry

Directions:

Read this excerpt from "Becky and the Wheels-and-Brake Boys" by James Berry. Then, complete numbers 9 and 10 by choosing the best answer.

Over and over I told my mum I wanted a bike. Over and over she looked at me as if I was crazy. "Becky, d'you think you're a boy? Eh? D'you think you're a boy? In any case, where's the money to come from? Eh?"

Of course I know I'm not a boy. Of course I know I'm not crazy. Of course I know all that's no reason why I can't have a bike. No reason! As soon as I get indoors I'll just have to ask again—ask Mum once more.

9 Which sentence best describes the literary point of view used in this passage?

A A third-person narrator describes the thoughts and actions of several other people.

B A first-person narrator describes only her own thoughts and actions.

C A first-person narrator describes her own thoughts and the actions of herself and others.

D A third-person narrator describes the action through the eyes of one person.

10 Becky's mother does not want her to have a bicycle because—

F she thinks only boys should ride bicycles.

G Becky does not do her chores.

H she wants Becky to watch her sister.

J Becky is too young.

Name ______________________________ Date ______________

Reading Comprehension

Directions:

Read this excerpt from a textbook. Then, complete number 11 by choosing the best answer.

The National Aeronautics and Space Administration (NASA) is responsible for running the United States space program. NASA's Project Mercury put the first Americans in space. This project also established NASA's ability to launch Earth-orbiting spacecraft. Project Apollo was designed to land Americans on the moon, a goal that was accomplished in July 1969 with the *Apollo 11* mission. Five additional lunar landings followed this success, ending with *Apollo 17* in 1972. As the space shuttle program continues, astronauts use their unique zero-gravity environment to conduct experiments and gather information for the benefit of earthbound humankind and future space travelers.

11 What is this passage mostly about?

A future space travelers

B the importance of the space shuttle

C astronauts' specialized training

D NASA's accomplishments

Name ______________________ Date ______________

Reading Comprehension

Directions:

Read the following poster. Then, complete number 12 by choosing the best answer.

The Middle View Area Ski Club will hold **a Ski Trip to Silver Bells Ski Resort** **on January 10** Students, friends, and family of all ages welcome! Bus leaves the school at 8:30 A.M. and returns at 10:30 P.M. Cost is $45 per person, including ski rental, lunch, and dinner. Tickets are available at the school office. The Ski Club needs your help! Students and parents need to organize and supervise the trip. Call Tony Parks at 555-2378 for more information.

12 Which of the following sentences from the poster is meant to persuade you to volunteer to organize the trip?

F Tickets are available at the school office.

G Call Tony Parks at 555-2378 for more information.

H The Ski Club needs your help!

J Bus leaves the school at 8:30 A.M. and returns at 10:30 P.M.

Name ____________________ Date ____________

Spelling

Directions:

Read each group of sentences. For each item on the answer sheet, fill in the bubble for the answer that has a mistake in spelling. If there is no mistake, fill in the last answer choice.

1 **A** Science is Lee's favorite subject.
B Are the tomatoes ripe yet?
C Valentine's Day is in Febuary.
D No mistake

2 **F** The secetary typed the letter.
G Most kittens are curious.
H Whales are mammals, not fish.
J No mistake

3 **A** Lucy ate ninety peanuts.
B The shirt was a bargin at $3.00.
C Parallel lines never meet.
D No mistake

4 **F** Answer all of the questions.
G We will buy a new calendar in December.
H Gary saw a movie at the theater.
J No mistake

5 **A** They ate lunch in the cafeteria.
B The next street is Sixth Avenue.
C Did you take medicin for your cold?
D No mistake

6 **F** Mom cooked spagetti and meatballs.
G Darla's birthday is on Wednesday.
H Would you like more mashed potatoes?
J No mistake

7 **A** Luke weighs 85 pounds.
B Is that word misspelled?
C It takes coperation to succeed.
D No mistake

8 **F** There was a mysterious noise in the woods.
G The boys paddled the canoe.
H In the fall the leaves change color.
J No mistake

9 **A** It is neccesary to finish high school.
B Sign the letter "Yours truly."
C Winter is Bart's favorite season.
D No mistake

10 **F** The fans shouted encouragement at the runners.
G The puppy excaped from the yard.
H Measure the width of the table.
J No mistake

11 **A** Abbreviate Alabama as AL.
B A drum is a rythm instrument.
C That restaurant serves tacos.
D No mistake

Name ______________________________ Date ______________

Spelling

12 F Do tests give you anxiety?

G Pay the cashier for your lunch.

H What is your opinon of rap music?

J No mistake

13 A An eclipse will ocurr tomorrow.

B Those scissors are very sharp.

C A nickel equals five cents.

D No mistake

14 F A censis counts all the people.

G He ate ice cream for dessert.

H The bride walked down the aisle.

J No mistake

15 A Look up the word in a dictionary.

B The Civil War was in the ninteenth century.

C How old will you be in ninety years?

D No mistake

16 F The ending of the book satisfied Selma.

G The ending surprised Rita.

H Brandon liked the eighth chapter best.

J No mistake

17 A The flower garden is beautiful.

B Let's take a photograph of the parade.

C It is impolite to interupt.

D No mistake

18 F 100 percent is the maximum score.

G Read the paragraf about Mars.

H Encyclopedia Brown is an amateur detective.

J No mistake

19 A A chameleon's color is changeable.

B Daily exercise helps make people healthy.

C Give the dog a biskit as a treat.

D No mistake

20 F Will you persue computers as a career?

G The actors rehearsed the play.

H Malik fell and bruised his knee.

J No mistake

21 A The physician looked at Sue's tonsils.

B Many scientists work in a labertory.

C Return the books to the library.

D No mistake

22 F The surprise party was a sucess.

G The pyramids are ancient tombs.

H A weather satellite orbits Earth.

J No mistake

Name ______________________ Date ______________

Language

Directions:

Read each passage. Then decide which type of error, if any, appears in each underlined section. For each item on the answer sheet, fill in the bubble for the answer. If there is no error, fill in the last answer choice.

<u>The worlds largest library is the Library of Congress,</u> (1) which is in Washington, D.C. The original <u>library was burned by british troops during</u> (2) the War of 1812. The federal <u>government had very little money to build a new one, but</u> (3) a former president stepped in to help. <u>Thomas Jefferson, donated more than six thousand of his own books</u> (4) to get the new library going. From this <u>humble begining, the Library of Congress has grown to include</u> (5) more than 20 million books, 10 million prints and photographs, and 4 million atlases and maps. <u>To hold these books, their are more than 530 miles of shelves.</u> (6)

1 **A** Spelling error
B Capitalization error
C Punctuation error
D No error

2 **F** Spelling error
G Capitalization error
H Punctuation error
J No error

3 **A** Spelling error
B Capitalization error
C Punctuation error
D No error

4 **F** Spelling error
G Capitalization error
H Punctuation error
J No error

5 **A** Spelling error
B Capitalization error
C Punctuation error
D No error

6 **F** Spelling error
G Capitalization error
H Punctuation error
J No error

Name ____________________ Date ____________

Language

Many people believe, that animals cannot see colors, but [7] this is not true. Dogs, horses, and sheep are able to see some colors, although not as well as Humans can. [8] Monkeys are able to see colors, to. In fact, their color [9] vision is almost equal to our own. It is also obvious that birds' can see colors. [10] There are different ways they attract other birds, one of these ways is through their [11] natural color.

But there are many animals that apparently cannot see colors. Bulls, for example, are probly not excited by the color red in a bullfighter's cape. [12] Instead, they are excited only by the movement of the cape in the bullfighter's hands. [13]

7 **A** Spelling error
B Capitalization error
C Punctuation error
D No error

8 **F** Spelling error
G Capitalization error
H Punctuation error
J No error

9 **A** Spelling error
B Capitalization error
C Punctuation error
D No error

10 **F** Spelling error
G Capitalization error
H Punctuation error
J No error

11 **A** Spelling error
B Capitalization error
C Punctuation error
D No error

12 **F** Spelling error
G Capitalization error
H Punctuation error
J No error

13 **A** Spelling error
B Capitalization error
C Punctuation error
D No error

Name ______________________________ Date ______________

Language

Directions:

Read the passage. Then, choose the word or group of words that belongs in each space. For each item on the answer sheet, fill in the bubble for the answer that you think is correct.

The writer Bailey White has an ___(1)___ story to tell of how, as a child, she hatched sixteen wild turkeys! White's mother had long been a friend of local ornithologists, or bird experts. The ornithologists were worried that the wild turkey was headed for extinction [dying out]. When they found a nest of eggs, they could hardly control their excitement. They camped out in the woods to protect the ___(2)___ nest from people or animals that might harm it. Unfortunately, however, they scared off the mother turkey, and she ___(3)___ her nest on the night the eggs were supposed to hatch.

Six-year-old Bailey White was suffering from a case of the measles and a temperature that ___(4)___ to 102 degrees. She barely remembers the ornithologists creeping into ___(5)___ room with a cardboard box, but she remembers very clearly what happened the next morning. When she woke up, the little girl was surprised to find sixteen baby turkeys ___(6)___ her bed! White helped take care of the turkeys until one day in late summer. Then, with the ornithologists and White ___(7)___ watching, the wild turkeys were set free.

1 **A** interested
B interesting
C interest
D interests

2 **F** rarest
G rarer
H rare
J rarely

3 **A** abandoned
B would have abandoned
C abandoning
D was abandoned

4 **F** had risen
G will rise
H rises
J is rising

5 **A** their
B her
C she
D our

6 **F** sharing
G are sharing
H share
J shares

7 **A** most careful
B careful
C carefully
D more careful

Name ______________________________ Date ______________

Language

Directions:

Read each passage. Some sections are underlined. The underlined sections may be one of the following:

- **Incomplete sentences**
- **Run-on sentences**
- **Correctly written sentences that should be combined**
- **Correctly written sentences that do not need to be rewritten**

Choose the best way to write each underlined section and mark the letter for your answer. If the underlined section needs no change, mark the choice "Correct as is."

<u>Without the hard work of Noah Webster. We might never have had spelling bees!</u> (8)
<u>In the early days of the United States no uniform spelling of words existed.</u> (9) <u>Webster changed all that with his *American Dictionary of the English Language.*</u> (10) <u>It was published in 1828. It included 70,000 words.</u> (11)

8 **F** Without the hard work of Noah Webster, we might never have had spelling bees!

G Without the hard work. Of Noah Webster we might never have had spelling bees!

H Without the hard work of Noah Webster, which we might never have had spelling bees!

J Correct as is

9 **A** In the early days of the United States. No uniform spelling of words existed.

B In the early days of the United States, no uniform spelling of words existed.

C No uniform spelling of words existed until the early days of the United States.

D Correct as is

10 **F** Webster changed all that. With his *American Dictionary of the English Language.*

G Webster, changed all that, with his *American Dictionary of the English Language.*

H Changing all that, Webster did with his *American Dictionary of the English Language.*

J Correct as is

11 **A** It was published in 1828 and the dictionary also included 70,000 words.

B Published in 1828, it included 70,000 words.

C It was published in 1828, it included 70,000 words.

D Correct as is

Name ______________________________ Date ______________

Language

It was spring of the year 1836. [12] The Texas Revolution had been going on for several months. It had started in October 1835. Many lives had already been lost. [13] The Texans had suffered a serious defeat at the Alamo mission. The Alamo was a mission in San Antonio. [14] The 189 men there had fought against more than 3,000 Mexican troops, and every one of them had died in the battle.

On April 21, 1836, the Texans' luck turned when Sam Houston's army crept up on the Mexican troops near the San Jacinto River. [15] There they sprang a surprise attack. Which turned out to be more successful than they had imagined. The Battle of San Jacinto lasted less than 20 minutes and ended when the Texans captured the Mexican leader, Santa Anna. [16] In return for setting him free, the Texans demanded their immediate independence. The Mexican leader had little choice but to agree. A treaty was quickly signed. [17] Texas was no longer part of Mexico it was an independent country.

12 **F** The Texas Revolution had been going on for several months, it had started in October 1835.

G The Texas Revolution had started in October 1835 and the Texas Revolution had been going on for several months.

H The Texas Revolution, which had started in October 1835, had been going on for several months.

J Correct as is

13 **A** The Alamo was a mission in San Antonio, which Texans had suffered a serious defeat there.

B The Texans had suffered a serious defeat at the Alamo mission in San Antonio.

C Suffering a serious defeat, the Alamo was a mission in San Antonio.

D Correct as is

Name ______________________________ Date ______________

Language

14 F The 189 men there had fought against more than 3,000 Mexican troops, every one of them had died in the battle.

G The 189 men there had fought. Against more than 3,000 Mexican troops, who had all died in the battle.

H Against more than 3,000 troops were what the 189 men had fought against and died there.

J Correct as is

15 A There they sprang a surprise attack and the surprise attack turned out to be more successful than they had imagined.

B There they sprang a surprise attack, which turned out to be more successful than they had imagined.

C They were more successful than they had imagined. When they sprang a surprise attack there.

D Correct as is

16 F In return for setting him free. The Texans demanded their immediate independence.

G In return, the Texans demanded their immediate independence, for setting him free.

H The Texans demanded their immediate independence, in return they set him free.

J Correct as is

17 A Texas was no longer part of Mexico; it was an independent country.

B Texas was no longer part of Mexico and Texas was an independent country.

C Texas, no longer part of Mexico, an independent country.

D Correct as is

Name ______________________ Date ______________

Language

Directions:

Read the following questions. Then, complete number 18 by choosing the best answer.

18 Suppose that you are writing an essay comparing your favorite class and your least favorite class. Which of the following organizers would be most useful?

F time line

G cause-effect frame

H Venn diagram

J character-change map

Directions:

Kenny is working on an essay about his pet hamster. Several mistakes need to be corrected. Read the following paragraph. Then, complete numbers 19 through 21 by choosing the best answer.

[1]When my brother and I asked our parents for a pet, we were hoping for a dog, so we were disappointed when our father bought us a hamster, but we weren't sad for long. [2]Sammy is our hamster. [3]Sammy is really cute. [4]He also spends a lot of time digging. [5]My father told my brother and me that Sammy does this because hamsters dig burrows in the wild. [6]Sammy is the most lovable hamster I have ever seen. [7]He loves to come out of his cage and be held. [8]Sometimes he crawls up my arm, onto my shoulder, and nibbles my ear. [9]Show me a dog do that!

19 Which of these best combines Sentences 2 and 3 into one?

A Sammy is our hamster, but he is really cute.

B Sammy is our hamster and really cute.

C Sammy is our hamster; Sammy is really cute.

D Sammy, our hamster, is really cute.

20 Which sentence should be rewritten as two complete sentences?

F Sentence 1

G Sentence 5

H Sentence 6

J Sentence 7

21 If Kenny wanted to add a paragraph to his essay, a good topic would be

A what hamsters eat

B what kind of dog Kenny wants

C why hamsters are cute

D who takes care of Sammy

Name ______________________ Date ______________

Answer Sheet

1.	Ⓐ	Ⓑ	Ⓒ	Ⓓ	31.	Ⓐ	Ⓑ	Ⓒ	Ⓓ
2.	Ⓕ	Ⓖ	Ⓗ	Ⓙ	32.	Ⓕ	Ⓖ	Ⓗ	Ⓙ
3.	Ⓐ	Ⓑ	Ⓒ	Ⓓ	33.	Ⓐ	Ⓑ	Ⓒ	Ⓓ
4.	Ⓕ	Ⓖ	Ⓗ	Ⓙ	34.	Ⓕ	Ⓖ	Ⓗ	Ⓙ
5.	Ⓐ	Ⓑ	Ⓒ	Ⓓ	35.	Ⓐ	Ⓑ	Ⓒ	Ⓓ
6.	Ⓕ	Ⓖ	Ⓗ	Ⓙ	36.	Ⓕ	Ⓖ	Ⓗ	Ⓙ
7.	Ⓐ	Ⓑ	Ⓒ	Ⓓ	37.	Ⓐ	Ⓑ	Ⓒ	Ⓓ
8.	Ⓕ	Ⓖ	Ⓗ	Ⓙ	38.	Ⓕ	Ⓖ	Ⓗ	Ⓙ
9.	Ⓐ	Ⓑ	Ⓒ	Ⓓ	39.	Ⓐ	Ⓑ	Ⓒ	Ⓓ
10.	Ⓕ	Ⓖ	Ⓗ	Ⓙ	40.	Ⓕ	Ⓖ	Ⓗ	Ⓙ
11.	Ⓐ	Ⓑ	Ⓒ	Ⓓ	41.	Ⓐ	Ⓑ	Ⓒ	Ⓓ
12.	Ⓕ	Ⓖ	Ⓗ	Ⓙ	42.	Ⓕ	Ⓖ	Ⓗ	Ⓙ
13.	Ⓐ	Ⓑ	Ⓒ	Ⓓ	43.	Ⓐ	Ⓑ	Ⓒ	Ⓓ
14.	Ⓕ	Ⓖ	Ⓗ	Ⓙ	44.	Ⓕ	Ⓖ	Ⓗ	Ⓙ
15.	Ⓐ	Ⓑ	Ⓒ	Ⓓ	45.	Ⓐ	Ⓑ	Ⓒ	Ⓓ
16.	Ⓕ	Ⓖ	Ⓗ	Ⓙ	46.	Ⓕ	Ⓖ	Ⓗ	Ⓙ
17.	Ⓐ	Ⓑ	Ⓒ	Ⓓ	47.	Ⓐ	Ⓑ	Ⓒ	Ⓓ
18.	Ⓕ	Ⓖ	Ⓗ	Ⓙ	48.	Ⓕ	Ⓖ	Ⓗ	Ⓙ
19.	Ⓐ	Ⓑ	Ⓒ	Ⓓ	49.	Ⓐ	Ⓑ	Ⓒ	Ⓓ
20.	Ⓕ	Ⓖ	Ⓗ	Ⓙ	50.	Ⓕ	Ⓖ	Ⓗ	Ⓙ
21.	Ⓐ	Ⓑ	Ⓒ	Ⓓ	51.	Ⓐ	Ⓑ	Ⓒ	Ⓓ
22.	Ⓕ	Ⓖ	Ⓗ	Ⓙ	52.	Ⓕ	Ⓖ	Ⓗ	Ⓙ
23.	Ⓐ	Ⓑ	Ⓒ	Ⓓ	53.	Ⓐ	Ⓑ	Ⓒ	Ⓓ
24.	Ⓕ	Ⓖ	Ⓗ	Ⓙ	54.	Ⓕ	Ⓖ	Ⓗ	Ⓙ
25.	Ⓐ	Ⓑ	Ⓒ	Ⓓ	55.	Ⓐ	Ⓑ	Ⓒ	Ⓓ
26.	Ⓕ	Ⓖ	Ⓗ	Ⓙ	56.	Ⓕ	Ⓖ	Ⓗ	Ⓙ
27.	Ⓐ	Ⓑ	Ⓒ	Ⓓ	57.	Ⓐ	Ⓑ	Ⓒ	Ⓓ
28.	Ⓕ	Ⓖ	Ⓗ	Ⓙ	58.	Ⓕ	Ⓖ	Ⓗ	Ⓙ
29.	Ⓐ	Ⓑ	Ⓒ	Ⓓ	59.	Ⓐ	Ⓑ	Ⓒ	Ⓓ
30.	Ⓕ	Ⓖ	Ⓗ	Ⓙ	60.	Ⓕ	Ⓖ	Ⓗ	Ⓙ

Name ______________________ Date ______________________

Answer Sheet

1. (A) (B) (C) (D)
2. (A) (B) (C) (D)
3. (A) (B) (C) (D)
4. (A) (B) (C) (D)
5. (A) (B) (C) (D)
6. (A) (B) (C) (D)
7. (A) (B) (C) (D)
8. (A) (B) (C) (D)
9. (A) (B) (C) (D)
10. (A) (B) (C) (D)
11. (A) (B) (C) (D)
12. (A) (B) (C) (D)
13. (A) (B) (C) (D)
14. (A) (B) (C) (D)
15. (A) (B) (C) (D)
16. (A) (B) (C) (D)
17. (A) (B) (C) (D)
18. (A) (B) (C) (D)
19. (A) (B) (C) (D)
20. (A) (B) (C) (D)
21. (A) (B) (C) (D)
22. (A) (B) (C) (D)
23. (A) (B) (C) (D)
24. (A) (B) (C) (D)
25. (A) (B) (C) (D)
26. (A) (B) (C) (D)
27. (A) (B) (C) (D)
28. (A) (B) (C) (D)
29. (A) (B) (C) (D)
30. (A) (B) (C) (D)
31. (A) (B) (C) (D)
32. (A) (B) (C) (D)
33. (A) (B) (C) (D)
34. (A) (B) (C) (D)
35. (A) (B) (C) (D)
36. (A) (B) (C) (D)
37. (A) (B) (C) (D)
38. (A) (B) (C) (D)
39. (A) (B) (C) (D)
40. (A) (B) (C) (D)
41. (A) (B) (C) (D)
42. (A) (B) (C) (D)
43. (A) (B) (C) (D)
44. (A) (B) (C) (D)
45. (A) (B) (C) (D)
46. (A) (B) (C) (D)
47. (A) (B) (C) (D)
48. (A) (B) (C) (D)
49. (A) (B) (C) (D)
50. (A) (B) (C) (D)
51. (A) (B) (C) (D)
52. (A) (B) (C) (D)
53. (A) (B) (C) (D)
54. (A) (B) (C) (D)
55. (A) (B) (C) (D)
56. (A) (B) (C) (D)
57. (A) (B) (C) (D)
58. (A) (B) (C) (D)
59. (A) (B) (C) (D)
60. (A) (B) (C) (D)

Name ______________________________ Date ____________________

Answer Sheet for ITBS

Vocabulary

1. Ⓐ Ⓑ Ⓒ Ⓓ	4. Ⓙ Ⓚ Ⓛ Ⓜ	7. Ⓐ Ⓑ Ⓒ Ⓓ	10. Ⓙ Ⓚ Ⓛ Ⓜ	13. Ⓐ Ⓑ Ⓒ Ⓓ
2. Ⓙ Ⓚ Ⓛ Ⓜ	5. Ⓐ Ⓑ Ⓒ Ⓓ	8. Ⓙ Ⓚ Ⓛ Ⓜ	11. Ⓐ Ⓑ Ⓒ Ⓓ	14. Ⓙ Ⓚ Ⓛ Ⓜ
3. Ⓐ Ⓑ Ⓒ Ⓓ	6. Ⓙ Ⓚ Ⓛ Ⓜ	9. Ⓐ Ⓑ Ⓒ Ⓓ	12. Ⓙ Ⓚ Ⓛ Ⓜ	

Reading Comprehension

1. Ⓐ Ⓑ Ⓒ Ⓓ	4. Ⓙ Ⓚ Ⓛ Ⓜ	7. Ⓐ Ⓑ Ⓒ Ⓓ	10. Ⓙ Ⓚ Ⓛ Ⓜ	13. Ⓐ Ⓑ Ⓒ Ⓓ
2. Ⓙ Ⓚ Ⓛ Ⓜ	5. Ⓐ Ⓑ Ⓒ Ⓓ	8. Ⓙ Ⓚ Ⓛ Ⓜ	11. Ⓐ Ⓑ Ⓒ Ⓓ	14. Ⓙ Ⓚ Ⓛ Ⓜ
3. Ⓐ Ⓑ Ⓒ Ⓓ	6. Ⓙ Ⓚ Ⓛ Ⓜ	9. Ⓐ Ⓑ Ⓒ Ⓓ	12. Ⓙ Ⓚ Ⓛ Ⓜ	

Spelling

1. Ⓐ Ⓑ Ⓒ Ⓓ Ⓔ	4. Ⓙ Ⓚ Ⓛ Ⓜ Ⓝ	7. Ⓐ Ⓑ Ⓒ Ⓓ Ⓔ	10. Ⓙ Ⓚ Ⓛ Ⓜ Ⓝ	13. Ⓐ Ⓑ Ⓒ Ⓓ Ⓔ
2. Ⓙ Ⓚ Ⓛ Ⓜ Ⓝ	5. Ⓐ Ⓑ Ⓒ Ⓓ Ⓔ	8. Ⓙ Ⓚ Ⓛ Ⓜ Ⓝ	11. Ⓐ Ⓑ Ⓒ Ⓓ Ⓔ	14. Ⓙ Ⓚ Ⓛ Ⓜ Ⓝ
3. Ⓐ Ⓑ Ⓒ Ⓓ Ⓔ	6. Ⓙ Ⓚ Ⓛ Ⓜ Ⓝ	9. Ⓐ Ⓑ Ⓒ Ⓓ Ⓔ	12. Ⓙ Ⓚ Ⓛ Ⓜ Ⓝ	

Capitalization

1. Ⓐ Ⓑ Ⓒ Ⓓ	4. Ⓙ Ⓚ Ⓛ Ⓜ	7. Ⓐ Ⓑ Ⓒ Ⓓ	10. Ⓙ Ⓚ Ⓛ Ⓜ	13. Ⓐ Ⓑ Ⓒ Ⓓ
2. Ⓙ Ⓚ Ⓛ Ⓜ	5. Ⓐ Ⓑ Ⓒ Ⓓ	8. Ⓙ Ⓚ Ⓛ Ⓜ	11. Ⓐ Ⓑ Ⓒ Ⓓ	
3. Ⓐ Ⓑ Ⓒ Ⓓ	6. Ⓙ Ⓚ Ⓛ Ⓜ	9. Ⓐ Ⓑ Ⓒ Ⓓ	12. Ⓙ Ⓚ Ⓛ Ⓜ	

Punctuation

1. Ⓐ Ⓑ Ⓒ Ⓓ	4. Ⓙ Ⓚ Ⓛ Ⓜ	7. Ⓐ Ⓑ Ⓒ Ⓓ	10. Ⓙ Ⓚ Ⓛ Ⓜ
2. Ⓙ Ⓚ Ⓛ Ⓜ	5. Ⓐ Ⓑ Ⓒ Ⓓ	8. Ⓙ Ⓚ Ⓛ Ⓜ	11. Ⓐ Ⓑ Ⓒ Ⓓ
3. Ⓐ Ⓑ Ⓒ Ⓓ	6. Ⓙ Ⓚ Ⓛ Ⓜ	9. Ⓐ Ⓑ Ⓒ Ⓓ	12. Ⓙ Ⓚ Ⓛ Ⓜ

Usage and Expression

1. Ⓐ Ⓑ Ⓒ Ⓓ	6. Ⓙ Ⓚ Ⓛ Ⓜ	11. Ⓐ Ⓑ Ⓒ Ⓓ	16. Ⓙ Ⓚ Ⓛ Ⓜ
2. Ⓙ Ⓚ Ⓛ Ⓜ	7. Ⓐ Ⓑ Ⓒ Ⓓ	12. Ⓙ Ⓚ Ⓛ Ⓜ	17. Ⓐ Ⓑ Ⓒ Ⓓ
3. Ⓐ Ⓑ Ⓒ Ⓓ	8. Ⓙ Ⓚ Ⓛ Ⓜ	13. Ⓐ Ⓑ Ⓒ Ⓓ	18. Ⓙ Ⓚ Ⓛ Ⓜ
4. Ⓙ Ⓚ Ⓛ Ⓜ	9. Ⓐ Ⓑ Ⓒ Ⓓ	14. Ⓙ Ⓚ Ⓛ Ⓜ	19. Ⓐ Ⓑ Ⓒ Ⓓ
5. Ⓐ Ⓑ Ⓒ Ⓓ	10. Ⓙ Ⓚ Ⓛ Ⓜ	15. Ⓐ Ⓑ Ⓒ Ⓓ	

Name ______________________ Date ______________

Answer Sheet for SAT 10

Vocabulary

1. A B C D	4. F G H J
2. F G H J	5. A B C D
3. A B C D	6. F G H J

Reading Comprehension

1. A B C D	6. F G H J	11. A B C D
2. F G H J	7. A B C D	12. F G H J
3. A B C D	8. F G H J	
4. F G H J	9. A B C D	
5. A B C D	10. F G H J	

Spelling

1. A B C D	6. F G H J	11. A B C D	16. F G H J	21. A B C D
2. F G H J	7. A B C D	12. F G H J	17. A B C D	22. F G H J
3. A B C D	8. F G H J	13. A B C D	18. F G H J	
4. F G H J	9. A B C D	14. F G H J	19. A B C D	
5. A B C D	10. F G H J	15. A B C D	20. F G H J	

Language

1. A B C D	5. A B C D	9. A B C D	13. A B C D
2. F G H J	6. F G H J	10. F G H J	
3. A B C D	7. A B C D	11. A B C D	
4. F G H J	8. F G H J	12. F G H J	

Language

1. A B C D	6. F G H J	11. A B C D	16. F G H J	21. A B C D
2. F G H J	7. A B C D	12. F G H J	17. A B C D	
3. A B C D	8. F G H J	13. A B C D	18. F G H J	
4. F G H J	9. A B C D	14. F G H J	19. A B C D	
5. A B C D	10. F G H J	15. A B C D	20. F G H J	

Listening

1. A B C D	4. F G H J
2. F G H J	5. A B C D
3. A B C D	

Answer Sheet

Short Answer/Essay